THE NEW ADVENTURES
OF ROBINSON CRUSOE

THE NEW ADVENTURES
OF ROBINSON CRUSOE

Norman Robbins

JOSEF WEINBERGER PLAYS

LONDON

THE NEW ADVENTURES OF ROBINSON CRUSOE
First published in 2015
by Josef Weinberger Ltd
12-14 Mortimer Street, London W1T 3JJ
www.josef-weinberger.com / plays@jwmail.co.uk

ISBN: 978 0 85676 353 3

Printed by Short Run Press Ltd, Exeter, Devon UK

For Tim and Pauline Kenyon . . . who love a good giggle.

AUTHOR'S NOTE

Robinson Crusoe was the first pantomime to boast a title familiar to today's audiences. Written 64 years after pantomime was invented by actor / manager John Rich, it was very loosely based on Daniel Defoe's famous novel by playwright / theatre manager and MP, Richard Brinsley Sheridan, for the Theatre Royal, Drury Lane, in 1781, and featured Giuseppe Grimaldi, (father of the famous Clown, Joseph Grimaldi) as Man Friday. Despite one critic proclaiming the script was "proof that even the greatest genius can sink beyond contempt," it was hugely successful and until the 1960s, various adaptations of the story played all over Britain, year after year.

Since then, however, the twin idiots of *Health and Safety* and *Political Correctness* have almost removed it from professional stagings. Their farcical rulings have systematically gnawed away at comic interludes of all pantomime subjects, and the lists of "Thou shalt not do, under pain of prosecution" grow longer every year. Even amateur companies are now being targeted, and more than one Society's annual panto has been cancelled a few days before opening, when local authorities who know little or nothing of its history have stepped in, quoting newly dreamed-up infractions or demanding changes to centuries-old storylines and routines.

I began my own version of *Robinson Crusoe* almost fifty years ago, but abandoned it when I realized what was happening. Other writers changed the plot line to avoid confrontation and / or prosecution, so many scripts now feature Blackbeard, the pirate, Long John Silver, Space Monsters or other so-called "attractions". To my mind, however, the original panto adventure has vanished, and though a few have made me laugh out loud, most have disappointed. The last *professional* version I saw, though packed with well-known television names, was deadly dull, verged on the obscene, and the audience appeared to agree as quite a number left at the interval. Personal feelings apart, it's a fact that we're seeing fewer productions of this famous panto every year, and it could very soon join the dozens of titles that have sunk into undeserved obscurity.

After sixty plus years as a writer / performer / director, and with dozens of successful scripts under my belt, I came to the conclusion that if *Robinson Crusoe* was to survive as a pantomime subject, a totally new adventure was needed. Something along the same lines, and still fully "traditional", but having almost nothing to do with the original version. Costumes and scenery could be adventures of their own, and the whole thing as audience-pleasing as Sheridan's original. This then, is the result. Written to celebrate the 300th birthday of pantomime (b. March 2nd, 1717), I sincerely hope you have as much fun performing it as I had when writing.

Norman Robbins

PRODUCTION NOTES

There should be no unforeseen problems. If scenery or costumes are to be hired, all are readily available from suppliers. With regard to properties, all can be knocked up by the average Stage Manager and his / her team at little cost. The Rod of Office for Codine could be an adapted snooker cue, and the treasure chests for the *Locker* scene would be effective if cut out of hardboard and painted up. The main treasure chest could be one of the old, easily obtainable, tin chests, painted up, and the padlock a simple cardboard cut-out.

The "Pelt" scenes were a very prominent feature of Georgian and Victorian pantomimes, and carried on right into the 1940s.

The vegetables, etc, used in the *opening* scene, should all be made from rags, polystyrene or plastic, and painted up. No one need get their skulls cracked with an under-ripe avocado. I've made *dozens* of such props over the past sixty years, so I know how easy it is to make them, and I'm no handyman. Any old chunks of polystyrene packaging are suitable for stage props. They can easily be cut to size, then rubbed to shape with a wire brush. Using a rubbery gum, cover the shapes with fine gauze and dry before painting with emulsion paint. Not Gloss. They'll last for *years*. A sharp knife, a small wire brush (such as a suede shoe brush), some Copydex and a few small pots of different coloured emulsion paints are all that's required (and make objects a little larger than life).

The rubbish for the *Ship* scene needs to be looked at in the same way. Banana skins can be made from yellow felt; tomatoes, etc, from polystyrene balls, painted up, while small cardboard cereal cartons, cleaned yogurt tubs, old slippers, etc, will give bulk. Fish carcasses can be made from cardboard, or polystyrene heads, painted up, cardboard tails, both joined up with a thickish drinking straw, pierced with nylon threads then trimmed to shape. Screwed up damp (not wet) newspaper, is also a good filler and has weight, but no sharp corners of edges. Buckets should be plastic and painted up. The important thing is that there should be plenty of this "rubbish". The stage should eventually be *awash* with it. The laughs get bigger with the amount. It's best to start collecting it together early in rehearsal time . . . and for the offstage crew, it's best tossed from plastic washing baskets.

Jewels for the treasure are Christmas tree decorations, gold and silver tinsel, and fruit pastilles and gums (you'll be surprised how good they look from the front). And old plastic beads sprayed various colors. Gold and silver cups, plates, etc, can be old china or tin sprayed up, and coins can be made from cardboard, or even chocolate coins can be used. No need for anything in the *main* chest to be seen, as it's closed most of the time, but a few overspills in the others will be effective.

The repulsive Sea Monster is whatever the costumier can come up with.

CAST OF CHARACTERS

DAVY JONES, *the Old Man of the Sea*

THE CORAL FAIRY

ROBINSON CRUSOE

HALE *and* HEARTY, *two dim-witted layabouts*

MRS CRUSOE, *Robinson's mother*

POLLY PERKINS, *Robinson's sweetheart*

BILLY CRUSOE, *Robinson's younger brother*

SIR PERCIVAL PENNYPINCH, *a miserly landowner*

QUEEN PARACETAMOL, *Ruler of Migrainia*

PRINCESS DISPRIN, *the Queen's daughter*

CODINE, *the Lord Chancellor*

SEA CREATURE

CHORUS OF CITIZENS, SAILORS, MIGRAINIANS, SEA SPIRITS, *etc.*

ACT ONE

ACT TWO

ACT ONE

Prologue: Davy Jones' Locker at the bottom of the sea.

A lane scene. The backdrop depicts a coral reef at the bottom of the sea, lit in subdued tones of green and red. DAVY JONES, *a fantastical and sinister figure swathed in seaweed of various hues, is C. He speaks in a growling, harsh voice.*

DAVY
Belay, all those who'd live afloat. Belay, and hark to me.
The Ruler of the Seas, am I. Old Davy Jones, I be.
I'm here to give yer warning fair. If you'd be safe, *stay home.*
For if I wants, I'll *sink* yer ships as o'er my realm you roam.
No vessel's been built yet, that can withstand the storms I raise.
Though some last but an hour or so (*Leers.*) some others last for days
With mighty waves and howling winds, I breach each ship's defenses . . .
Intending soon, to be as rich as Politicians on expenses. (*Laughs harshly.*)
Oh, yes . . . yer treasure's what I want. Each day I crave for more.
For *centuries* I've stolen it from sunken wrecks galore. (*With menace.*)
But don't go thinkin' *you've* a chance of finding where it lies . . .
For mark my words, just try it, and you'll get a *big* surprise.
In short, if on the seas you'd sail, you'd be quite off your rocker
To ignore old Davy Jones' advice. (*Snarls.*) And end up in my *Locker.*
(*Laughs harshly.*)

(*Enter* THE CORAL FAIRY, *R., in a white follow-spot.*)

FAIRY
Oh, dear. Your loud and boastful claim
To rule the ocean lands,
Is quite *untrue.* It rests, (and always *has* done),
In King Neptune's kindly hands.
At *his* command, I'm here to put a stop to your sad game.
A task I'll do most willingly. The Coral Fairy is my name. (*Curtsies.*)

DAVY
(*Scornfully.*) King Neptune. Bah. He's old and weak
Unfit to wear the crown.
Each ship-wrecked sailor *he* would save,
Whilst *I* prefer to see them *drown.*
So do yer worst. But mark my words, yer won't succeed. You'll fail.
This very morn, from Port of Hull, *"The Jellied Eel"* intends to sail.

Laden down with coins of gold, that shortly shall be *mine*.
(*Gleefully*.) For all on board shall *perish* 'ere the moon begins to shine.

FAIRY
Not so. For I know *one* brave soul,
Who'll outwit *you* with ease.
And though your storms may sink that ship,
He'll bring you to your bony knees.
Upon a desert island once, marooned 'til rescue came,
Your nemesis is home again. And *Robinson Crusoe* is his name.

DAVY
(*Amused*.) Don't make me laugh. A *mortal* who will get the best of *me?*
(*To audience*.) This fairy's lost her marbles.

FAIRY
Oh? You'll see, my friend. You'll see.
But just for now, it's time, I think, for *you* to disappear.
I'm sure the audience agrees, you're *quite* unwelcome here.

DAVY
(*Sneers*.) Suits me. An uglier, gormless lot,
I've never seen, I swear.
It hurts me just to look at 'em. (*Selects a "victim" in the audience*.)
Especially, that one there . . . (*Indicates generally*.)
But *all* of them are *horrible*. They're absolutely *thick*.
So somewhere else will suit me fine. I'll go, before I'm *sick*.

>   (*He grimaces at audience and exits L. rapidly. The
>   green light goes out*.)

FAIRY
Such *rudeness*. And, as well we know, his words are *quite* untrue.
So every time he shows his face, I think you all should loudly *Boo*.
But just for now, ignore his threats. I give you all my word,
No harm shall come to anyone. His plans are quite absurd.
In merriment, our time we'll spend. So let this tale begin.
To Hull's great port, we'll go, where stands the famous *Mermaid Inn*,
And honest Townsfolk work and thrive
In this Year of Grace . . . Seventeen O Five.

>   (*Waves her wand. There is an instant blackout*. FAIRY *exits
>   R. in the darkness and lane curtain opens to reveal* . . .)

Scene One: The City of Hull.

A full scene. Typical pantomime backdrop of half-timbered buildings, perhaps with a glimpse of ships' masts and wooded cliffs in the distance behind the buildings. Masking entrances and exits L. and R., are portions of quaint cottages, The Mermaid Inn, and a Chandler's shop. None of these need be practical, but if space is available, can be utilized by the director. When the scene begins, it is daylight, and CITIZENS *and* SAILORS *are singing and dancing.*

MUSIC No. 1. (CITIZENS *and* SAILORS)

Midway through the song, ROBINSON CRUSOE *enters C.B., moving through the group to C.F. and joining in. He is a dashing young man in tights, baggy-sleeved shirt, sleeveless tunic, and wears a small peaked hat with a jaunty feather in it. At the end of the song, all but* ROBINSON *and* TWO CITIZENS *move back to form small groups, some of whom chat animatedly but silently, whilst others observe and react.*

CITIZEN 1
(*To* ROBINSON.) And who's got a smile on *his* face, this morning?

ROBINSON
(*Brightly.*) Why shouldn't I have? It's a wonderful day . . . I've been offered a job on *The Jellied Eel*, and we'll be sailing just before noon.

CITIZEN 2
(*Shocked.*) Robinson *Crusoe.* It's less than a week since you were rescued from that desert island after being lost for goodness knows how many years, and now you're leaving *again?* What about Polly Perkins? I don't think *she'll* be too happy about it. You've only just got *engaged.*

ROBINSON
(*Wryly.*) I know. But unless I find work, we can't *afford* to get married. And there's not a job to be had in Hull *these* days.

CITIZEN 1
(*Nodding.*) That's true. Most of *us* have been out of work for weeks. But (*Names Prime Minister*)'s just announced he's found a way of making the unemployment lines *much* shorter.

ROBINSON
(*Interested.*) What's that?

CITIZEN 1
We have to stand closer together.

(*All laugh.*)

ROBINSON
(*Amused.*) Oh, well . . . if that's the best he can do, I'd better carry on
with my packing. And after that, I *must* find mother and tell her I'm
leaving. You've not seen her around, have you?

(*All shake their heads.*)

(*Puzzled.*) Where on earth can she have got to? She only went out to do
some shopping. (*Brightly.*) Still . . . I'm sure she'll turn up before we
sail. And if not, I'll just have to leave her a note.

CITIZEN 2
So where are you going on *The Jellied Eel?*

ROBINSON
I haven't a clue. All I know is it's *somewhere* in the world, and the owner
says if I *work* hard, when I get back home again, my pockets will be
bulging with gold.

(*Everyone looks amused.*)

CITIZEN 2
That's the same story you were told *years* ago. And what happened? You
ended up shipwrecked, and came home with nothing but Man Friday.

ROBINSON
(*Fondly.*) Ah. Dear old Man Friday. I wonder how he's getting on in his
new job.

CITIZEN 1
(*Surprised.*) New job? But he can't read or write, *or* count above ten.
What job can *he* do?

ROBINSON
He's an Advisor to (*Local County Council*).

(*All laugh.*)

CITIZEN 2
They *do* say the streets of London are paved with gold. Why not go there instead? It's a lot closer than abroad.

ROBINSON
True . . . but I want *adventure* as well. (*Expansively.*) I want to *explore* strange lands, meet foreign people and see their great cities. (*Excitedly.*) Can't you *imagine* it? A week in China . . . a month in Africa . . . a year in America.

CITIZEN 1
And the rest of your life in *debt*.

(*All laugh.*)

ROBINSON
(*Lightly.*) Oh, you can laugh, but today's the start of a new life for *me*, and once we've set sail, the world's going to be my oyster.

MUSIC No. 2. (ROBINSON *and* CHORUS)

(*As the song ends,* ROBINSON *exits happily and the others gradually disperse L. and R. As they do so* SIR PERCIVAL PENNYPINCH *enters down R. He is a cantankerous old man, dressed to the height of fashion, and walks with the aid of a stout cane.*)

SIR PERCY
(*Chuckling with glee.*) Just a few more hours afore *The Jellied Eel* sets sail, and the tax collectors haven't a clue I'll be hiding a fortune from 'em. (*Bitterly.*) Why should *I* pay taxes on me money? I've had to *work* for it. (*Musing.*) Oh, *yes.* I remember the days *afore* I became Sir Percival Pennypinch. All I had in the world were *five p* . . . But I knew wi' *my* brains and a bit of hard work . . . one day I'd be the richest man in Yorkshire. So I'll tell yer what I did. (*Confidentially.*) I bought a scabby lookin' apple with it . . . then polished and polished and polished it 'til it shone just like a *mirror* (*Proudly.*) and sold it fer *ten p*. Quick as a flash, I bought two more and did the same wi' them, and afore I knew it, I'd a whole *basketful* of apples. (*Smugly.*) After *that,* it were easy . . . my rich *Uncle* died and left me twenty-eight million pounds. (*Chortles, then scowls.*) Trouble is, the government's bin trying to get its hands on it ever since. (*Brightening.*) But now I've taken legal advice an' found a way ter *diddle* 'em. Me ship's laden with all the gold I've been hiding, an' soon it'll be resting in a foreign bank where no one can touch it but *me.* (*Scowls again.*) Only problem is . . . I'm still short of crew who are

too thick to ask questions, and time's a-passing. If I'm going to catch the tide, I have to work fast. (*Exits down L.*)

> (*As he does so,* HALE *and* HEARTY *enter C.B. and move down C.F. They are dressed in scruffy, ill-fitting pantaloons, garish stockings, bright baggy shirts and sleeveless tunics. Both wear soft wide-brimmed hats that have seen better days.*)

HALE
(*Looking around delightedly.*) Oooooh, here we are, Hearty. The Port of Hull. We're bound to find work here.

HEARTY
(*Beaming.*) I know. I know. And just think. Once we've earned some money, we can buy some new shirts.

HALE
What do we want new shirts for? We've only been wearing these for *ten* years. Give 'em a wash, and they'll last another *twenty.*

HEARTY
No fear. I'm not washing *anything* from now on. Especially if I've got to do it in one of them daft washing machines they've just invented. They don't *work* properly.

HALE
What do you mean, they don't work properly?

HEARTY
Well . . . there was one in the bathroom of that place I stayed in last week, so I lifted the lid, (*Doing the actions.*) put all my dirty washing inside, pressed the little lever down, and I've not seen it since.

HALE
(*After a reaction.*) Were you *born* stupid, or did you have to learn it?

HEARTY
(*Indignantly.*) Who are *you* calling stupid? I come from a brainy family, I do. (*Proudly.*) My *dad* was a famous inventor. He once crossed an elephant with a wasp.

HALE
(*Interested.*) And what did he call it?

HEARTY
I don't know . . . but it didn't half hurt when it stung you.

> (HALE *snatches his hat off and beats* HEARTY *around the shoulders with it.*)

Owww. Owww.

HALE
(*Putting his hat back on.*) I don't know why I *bother* with you. I bet you've never even *seen* an elephant

HEARTY
Yes, I have. Yes, I have.

HALE
All right, then. What's the difference between a fully grown elephant and a tiny little mouse?

HEARTY
About two *tons.*

HALE
(*Defeated.*) I give up. Trying to get sense out of *you's* like trying to get milk from a cat.

HEARTY
My uncle *Fred* can do that. Get milk from a cat.

HALE
(*Incredulously.*) Don't be daft. How can *anyone* get milk from a *cat*?

HEARTY
By pinching its saucer. (*Chortles.*)

> (HALE *snatches his hat off again and batters* HEARTY *with it.*)

Owww. Owww. Owww.

> (HALE *replaces his hat.*)

Whatcher keep doing *that* for? I've got bruises all down my equilibrium.

HALE

Yes. Well I'm going to *keep* doing it, 'til I can knock some *sense* into you. How can we find jobs if *you* keep making stupid remarks? People will think we're barmy. Now come on. We'll go into that cafe over there (*Indicates vaguely.*) and get something to eat before we go to the Job Centre.

> (*They exit down R., chatting amiably. As they do so, There are a few bars of raucous music, and* MRS CRUSOE *enters up R., and makes her way C.F. She is a lady of uncertain age, wears an outrageous dress and carries an empty shopping bag.*)

MRS CRUSOE

(*Cheerfully.*) Hello, dears. Crusoe's the name. *Diphtheria* Crusoe. (*Coyly.*) Sweet sixteen, slim as a garden rake and widow of this parish. (*Simpers, then glares acidly at someone in the audience.*) Artistic *licence*, dear. Artistic *licence*. (*To audience, disgustedly.*) Oooh, there's always *one*, isn't there? Ready to contradict before you've even had time to open your mouth. I wouldn't mind, but she's not perfect herself. Talk about *jealous*. They took her husband into hospital last week with a broken leg, and she's done nothing but moan about it, ever since. "What's wrong with you?" I said. "He's getting better, isn't he?" "Well, yes," she said. "But every morning, a strange woman goes into see him, and makes him drink bottles and bottles of Coca Cola, and I want to know who she *is*." "Well, you needn't be jealous of her," I said. "She's only his fizzy-o-therapist." (*Beaming.*) Oh, but it's nice, isn't it? Having the place full of friendly faces. I know the feller over there, for instance. (*Indicates vaguely.*) Plays rugby for (*Names local rugby club.*) Yes. I met him in (*Local supermarket.*) last week, and asked him what *position* he played in. "Oh," he said. "Sort of crouched and bent over, like this." (*Does the action then glances somewhere else.*) Oh, and look who else is here. It's the couple from number seven. (*Confidentially to others.*) *Usually* they only go to West End theatres. I saw them last week in (*Local coffee shop.*) and asked them if they'd seen anything recently. "Oh, yes," she said, "We saw a play in London that had been published on the Internet." "Oh," I said. "And did it have a happy ending?" "Well," she said . . . "*We* were happy when it ended." Mind you . . . I don't know why I'm standing here *chatting*. I've not done my shopping yet. Oooh, and isn't life changing on the High Street, girls? I don't know about *yours*, but *ours* is full of Charity Shops. Not that I'm complaining. You can pick up all sorts of things for practically nothing. I bought a painting and a violin there last week for under a pound. I couldn't *believe* it when I took them along to the Antiques Road Show, and a feller there told me what they *were*. "Good Heavens," he said "That's a Picasso and a Stradivarius." (*Beaming.*) What do you think to *that*, boys and girls? A Picasso and a Stradivarius for under a pound. "And how much are they worth?" I asked him. "Well," he said . . . "Not a lot, really. Stradivarius was a *lousy* painter, and Picasso hadn't a *clue* about violins."

> (*Enter* POLLY PERKINS *up L. She is a very pretty girl with lots of charm and personality.*)

POLLY
(*Moving down F.*) Mrs Crusoe?

MRS CRUSOE
(*Looking.*) Oh, I say . . . it's me son's sweetheart . . . Polly Perkins. The second prettiest girl in Hull. (*Simpers, then beams at her.*)

POLLY
(*Smiling.*) You've not seen *Robinson*, have you? I can't find him anywhere.

MRS CRUSOE
Typical man, dear. Typical man. Just like a log fire.

POLLY
(*Puzzled.*) All warm and comforting?

MRS CRUSOE
No. If you don't keep your eye on 'em, they go out. But it's funny you should say you can't find him, because I'm looking for him myself. I want him to go down to the pet shop and give the manager a telling off.

POLLY
Why? What's happened?

MRS CRUSOE
Well . . . you know how he came back from that desert island last week with a parrot and Man Friday?

POLLY
Yes.

MRS CRUSOE
Well . . . Now Man Friday's *gone* . . . and taken the parrot *with* him . . . I've been feeling a bit *lonely*, so I thought I'd buy myself a budgeridgigar to cheer meself up. But when I got to the pet shop he'd *sold* them all,

and the only thing he had left was one of them birds with the big yellow
beaks. You know? A *Toucan.*

POLLY
(*Delightedly.*) Oh, I *love* Toucans, Mrs Crusoe. They're *beautiful.*

MRS CRUSOE
That's what *I* thought, as well. So I told him I'd *have* one. "Ah," he said
. . . "But they're very expensive, Toucans are. Can you *afford* it?" I said,
"Never you mind, you cheeky thing. Just send me the *bill.*" And he said,
"Not likely, Missis. It's the *whole* bird or *nothing.*"

POLLY
(*Amused.*) Oh, you *do* make me laugh, Mrs Crusoe. But I *must* find
Robinson before his ship sails.

MRS CRUSOE
(*Puzzled.*) What are you talking about? You wouldn't catch my Robinson
on a ship *these* days. Coming home from that desert island nearly
finished him off. The Captain shouted "All hands on deck," and some
idiot trod on his fingers.

POLLY
(*Dismayed.*) You mean . . . he hasn't he *told* you yet?

MRS CRUSOE
Told me? He's hardly had time to say *anything* since he got back.
Besides . . . why's he want to go sailing off again? Last night on the
television, they said Britain had the highest standard of living in the
world.

POLLY
(*Surprised.*) *Really?*

MRS CRUSOE
Yes. The only trouble is . . . most of us can't *afford* it. Look at *me,*
for instance. (*Tearfully.*) I'm so poor I can't buy meself a new pair of
shoes. I have to paint my feet black and lace up my toes.

POLLY
(*Dismayed.*) Oh, don't be upset, Mrs Crusoe. He's only trying to earn
enough to pay off your debts, and marry *me.* I'm sure he *was* going to
tell you. In fact he *migh*t be looking for you now.

MRS CRUSOE
(*Brightening.*) Oooh, I never thought of that. Quick. Let's get back to the
house and see if he's there.

> (*They exit down R. As they do so, the lights fade as* DAVY
> JONES *enters L. in a green spotlight.*)

DAVY
(*Sneering.*) Boo all yer like, you ugly lot. It doesn't bother me.
Despite that fairy's useless threats, I'm *still* the ruler of the sea.
And once *The Jellied Eel's* set sail upon its lengthy trek . . .
'Twill only take a *moment* to transform it to a *wreck*. (*Cackles.*)
(*Sourly.*) But first, I have to find this lad of whom the fairy spoke.
I don't intend to have *my* plans upset by some North Country bloke.
Ere long, he'll rest beneath the waves, with seaweed round his bones.
For no one ever gets the best of Mr Davy Jones.

> (*Cackles with glee and exits L. The green spot goes out
> and the lights return to normal. As they do so, there
> is loud angry shouting from a crowd off R., and* BILLY
> CRUSOE *enters up R., in a hail of carrots, fish, oranges,
> cabbages and turnips, etc. He is a zany character in
> bright outlandish clothing and has an irrepressible
> sense of humour. He hurries down C.F. as the hail
> diminishes.*)

BILLY
(*Grinning.*) Hiya, kids. (*Chortles.*) I went into Tesco's and shouted *Aldi*,
and look at all the stuff they've thrown at me. We won't have to buy
anything for dinner tonight, now, 'cos I got it all for nothing. My Mum'll
be ever so pleased. Well . . . she's always short of money and sometimes
we don't *have* enough for food. All we had yesterday was prune and
rhubarb casserole with syrup of figs sauce. Still . . . it kept us going for
a while. (*Remembers.*) Oh . . . but you don't know who I am, do you? I've
not introduced myself, yet. Well, my name's *Billy* Crusoe, and I live in a
little house over there (*Indicates R.*) with my Mum and my big brother,
Robinson. Have you met 'em yet? (*Audience reaction.*) You have?
(*Beams.*) They're smashing, aren't they? Especially Robinson. Ever since
we were little, he's shared everything he had with me. Mumps. Measles.
Chicken pox. Mind you, (*Glances around to check no one is listening.*)
he's a bit on the *funny* side. I bet *you* haven't got a big brother who
wears false eyelashes, lipstick, fish-net stockings and high heels. And
everybody says *I'm* daft, but I'm not as daft as *him*. He got shipwrecked
a few years ago, and had to swim for his life covered in blue and
red paint. It was only when he got to an island he realised he'd been

marooned. (*Chortles.*) Still . . . he's got a better memory than I have. I can't remember my own *name*, sometimes. I have to write it down on a piece of paper and keep it in my pocket in case somebody asks. If only there was a way . . . (*Realises.*) Here . . . I've just had an *idea.* If every time I come on I shout "Hiya kids," *you* could shout back "Hiya, Billy," and then I'd remember who I am. Will you *do* that? (*Audience response.*) Smashing. I'll tell you what, then. We'll have a little *practice.* I'll go off, and when I come back I'll shout "Hiya, kids," and you shout back "Hiya, Billy," as loud as you can. (*Exits down R., then re-enters.*) Hiya, kids.

> (*Audience response.*)

(*Brightly.*) Did you do it? Did you shout?

> (*Audience response.*)

(*Scornfully.*) No, you *didn't.* You never opened your *mouths.* I didn't hear a dicky-bird. Let's have another go.

> (*Repeats action until satisfied with the volume.*)

(*Beaming.*) That's better. I can *hear* you now. Well now we've got that out of the way, I'd better be getting back home with all this food. I wonder if I can find somebody to help me pick it all up?

> (*Enter* CHORUS, *L. and R. who react with delight at the sight of it all, quickly pick it up and hurry off happily.*)

(*Dismayed.*) Here. Come back That's mine, that is. Come back. (*To audience.*) Well, of all the cheek. I've nothing left now. (*Brightening.*) Still . . . They probably need it more than I do. And if it makes 'em happy, that's all that matters. All *I* want is for *everybody* to be happy.

MUSIC No. 3 (BILLY)

> (*After the song, which the* CHORUS *could join in if required, he exits up R. as the lights fade and the lane curtain closes to end the scene.*)

Scene Two: A Quiet Street.

A lane scene. Full lighting. HALE *and* HEARTY *enter L. and move C.*

HALE
(*Scowling.*) Well I didn't think much of *that* meal. When the waiter brought the steak I ordered, it was only *half cooked*. "Oy," I said. "Didn't you hear me say *"Well done?"*

HEARTY
And what did he say?

HALE
He said, "Thanks, mate. It's not often I get compliments." And *another* thing . . . There were maggots in that steak. Dozens and dozens of *maggots*.

HEARTY
(*Pulling a face.*) Oo-er. Didn't you complain to the manager?

HALE
Of course I did. "Look at that steak," I said, "It's crawled off my plate and it's creeping down the table."

HEARTY
So what did he do?

HALE
(*Indignantly.*) He didn't do *anything*. Just told me to wait at the end and catch it as it passed.

HEARTY
(*Sympathetically.*) Oooh. You should have had the same as *me*. I eatened *five* big greasy *pork sausages*. (*Smacks his lips.*)

HALE
(*After a pitying look.*) You did *what*?

HEARTY
(*Happily.*) Eatened five big greasy pork sausages.

HALE
(*Pointedly.*) You mean ate. *Ate*.

HEARTY
(*Frowning.*) Well, it *could* have been eight. I know there was a *lot*.

HALE
(*Wincing.*) You know what *your* trouble is, don't you? You're stupid. (*Prods him backwards on the next three words.*) Stupid, stupid, *stupid*.

HEARTY
(*Indignantly.*) No, I'm not.

HALE
Yes you are. The last time you went *swimming*, you left your *socks* on.

HEARTY
(*Defensively.*) Only 'cos the water was cold. And anyway . . . *you've* some need to talk. What happened when the Golf Club said you couldn't join until you'd played thirty-six holes? You bought a mouth organ.

HALE
(*Changing the subject.*) Yes. Well never mind *that*. Now we've got no money left, we've got to find jobs or we'll *starve* to death.

(*Enter* SIR PERCY *L. They do not notice him, but argue silently.*)

SIR PERCY
(*To audience.*) What's this? Two down and outs, lookin' fer work? *And* not too bright, by the looks of 'em. I'll sign 'em up, afore they gets away. (*Calling to* HALE *and* HEARTY.) Belay, there, me hearties. Belay.

(*They turn to see him.*)

HEARTY
Blimey. It's (*Well known unpopular personage.*)

SIR PERCY
So . . . (*Crosses to them, leering.*) Yer looking for *work*, are yer? Well how about workin' for *me?*

HALE
(*Doubtfully.*) Oooh, I don't know. We only work for fellers who are rich and powerful.

SIR PERCY
Then I'm just the one yer looking for. (*Proudly.*) Ain't nobody richer than Sir Percival Pennypinch. (*Puts his arm around* HEARTY's *shoulder.*) And as for *powerful* . . . I've only to say the *word*, and dozens of men can die. (*Smiles at him.*)

HEARTY
(*Reeling.*) I'm not surprised. Your breath smells *terrible*. (*Pulls free.*) Don't you use *toothpaste?*

SIR PERCY
(*Scowling.*) What for? None of me teeth are *loose*. 'Sides . . . me last
wife had a nasty *experience* through using *toothpaste*. She tried one of
them *fancy* kinds that has red stripes running through the middle of it.

HALE
And didn't it work?

SIR PERCY
Sort of. Ev'ry other tooth went red. (*Snarling.*) Now do yer want them
jobs, or don't yer?

HALE
(*Hastily.*) All right. All right. We'll *take* 'em. But what do we have to *do?*

SIR PERCY
(*Leering.*) Just listen to *me*, and I'll *tell* yer. But first, I need to know
how *tough* you are. Do yer know how to use yer fists?

HEARTY
Oh, yes. I used to be a boxer, I did. When I finished my *last* fight, the
referee presented me with a *cup.*

SIR PERCY
Fer knocking the other man out?

HALE
No. To keep his teeth in as he picked 'em up.

SIR PERCY
(*Scowling.*) Maybe meeting you two *wasn't* a good idea? (*Reluctantly.*)
Still . . . Beggars can't be choosers. If I takes *you* two, I only need three
more crew fer me ship, afore I sets sail fer foreign places.

HEARTY
You want us to work on a *ship?* (*Doubtfully.*) Oooh, I don't know about
that. Is it well paid?

SIR PERCY
Fourpence a week . . . *between* yer.

HALE
(*In disbelief.*) Fourpence a week? Between us? (*Sternly.*) You should be
ashamed of yourself. A rich feller like *you*. That's a *poultry* wage, that
is. Absolutely *poultry.*

SIR PERCY
(*Correcting him.*) Yer means *paltry.*

HEARTY
No, he doesn't. What *you're* offering's *chicken-feed.*

SIR PERCY
(*Scowling.*) Oh, all right, then. I'll pay you twopence each.

HALE
(*Beaming.*) That's better. (*Excitedly to* HEARTY.) And when we get back, we'll probably have enough money saved to find a Sports shop and get fitted out with all the latest *sports* gear.

HEARTY
(*Startled.*) Not *me.* My *brother* did that when he won the Lottery. He wanted to look like Andy Murray, (*Or other well known tennis player.*) and they sold him a pair of tennis shorts for five hundred pounds, a tennis shirt for a *thousand* pounds, some tennis shoes for *two thousand* pounds, and a tube of tennis balls for *three thousand* pounds. "Do you want anything else?" they asked him. "Oh, yes," he said. "I'd like a racquet." So they sold him the *shop.*

SIR PERCY
Bah. Enough of this badinage. If it's cash yer wanting, then follow *me.* By this time next week, you'll be up to yer *necks* in money.

HALE / HEARTY
(*Together.*) Ooooooh. *Money.*

MUSIC No. 4 (HALE, HEARTY *and* SIR PERCY)

> (*At the end of the song, they exit and the lane curtain opens onto . . .*)

Scene Three: The Quayside.

Full scene. A great port, with ships, buildings, and perhaps a sea wall. Rough looking SAILORS *are busy loading the ship, moving on and offstage with their burdens.* CITIZENS *are watching and enjoying the sight.*

MUSIC No. 5 (CHORUS / DANCERS)

(At the end of the song / dance, the stage clears gradually and MRS CRUSOE, *enters up R., in a new and outrageous outfit.)*

MRS CRUSOE
(Concerned.) Ooh, I say. I've looked all over for Robinson, and there's not a sign of him anywhere. You don't think he's gone already, do you? Sailed away without a word to his poor old mum? *(Sobs.)* Ooooh, I might never see him again.

(Enter BILLY, *L.)*

BILLY
(To audience.) Hiya, kids. *(Audience response.)* Hiya, Mum.

MRS CRUSOE
(Eagerly.) Ooooh, Billy. You've not seen your big brother, have you?

BILLY
No. And I want to ask him if he'll take me to the zoo.

MRS CRUSOE
I shouldn't bother. If they want you, they'll come and get you.

BILLY
Har, har, Very funny. But I'm glad you're here, Mum. Do you remember that *apple* you gave me this morning? That great big *red* one, that was all full of juice that dribbled right down my chin when I sank my teeth in it?

MRS CRUSOE
Oh, yes. I remember *that*. I spent half an hour mopping the floor, afterwards.

BILLY
Yes. Well can you give me 50p for another one? I'm *starving*.

MRS CRUSOE
(Shocked.) Another apple? You must be joking. Do you think they grow on *trees?* Anyway . . . I *can't* give you 50p. I need all my money for the Travel Agent. *(Beams.)* I've decided to go to the Capital City of China for me holidays.

BILLY
(Surprised.) Pekin?

Mrs Crusoe
No. I want a *real* look round.

Billy
(*Disgusted.*) Well it's all right for *you*, isn't it? Going to *China* for your holidays. I suppose *we'll* be left here living on beans on toast, while *you're* having meals on board one of them floating restaurants in the harbour.

Mrs Crusoe
(*Primly.*) No I won't. I never eat junk foods. (*Musing.*) Mind you . . . I suppose I'll have to get the doctor to give me a check-up before I go. I don't want to be poorly while I'm there. (*Firmly.*) But I'm not going to the one down the road.

Billy
Why not?

Mrs Crusoe
Because your father saw *him* when he thought he was turning into a pair of curtains. And all he *did* was tell him to pull himself together.

(*Enter* Robinson, *L.*)

Robinson
Oh, *there* you are, mother. I've been looking all over for you. I've got *wonderful* news. I've been offered a job on *The Jellied Eel* and we sail today on the morning tide. By this time next week, I'll be halfway round the world.

Mrs Crusoe
(*Glowering.*) I've already *heard.* And what I want to know is how you got a job on a *ship?* They've changed all the rules, since the *last* time you went gallivanting. You can't just stroll up saying "I want to be a sailor," *nowadays.* You've got to answer *questions.*

Robinson
But I *did.* The owner asked me how many legs a *cow* had.

Mrs Crusoe
Well I don't know what *that's* got to do with being a sailor. (*Curious.*) What did you tell him?

Robinson
(*Smiling.*) Why, *four,* of course. And then he asked how many *horns* a cow had, and finally, he wanted to know how many *eyes* it had . . .

BILLY
(*Puzzled.*) Blimey. Hadn't he ever *seen* a cow?

MRS CRUSOE
(*Sighing.*) Well if you've *got* to go, I suppose you *have* to. I just hope you've packed clean underclothes, in case you get knocked down by a passing ship. Oh . . . and you'd better take some tablets in case you get seasick.

BILLY
Have *you* ever been seasick, Mum?

MRS CRUSOE
Seasick? I saw that film about the *Titanic* once, and felt so poorly they had to take me into the manager's office and call a doctor. (*Disgustedly.*) Not that *he* was much *use*.

ROBINSON
(*Surprised.*) Why not?

MRS CRUSOE
They'd put me on a green chair, and nobody could *find* me. (*Remembers.*)

BILLY
(*Wistfully.*) I wish *I* could sail round the world.

ROBINSON
Well I know the owner needs three more *crew*. If you *like*, I can ask if he'll take you on.

BILLY
(*Excitedly.*) Oooh. Can I go, Mum? Can I go?

MRS CRUSOE
(*Sharply.*) No, you can't. What'd happen if you got shipwreckedted? You can't swim a *stroke*. You'd be drowned in wetness.

BILLY
No, I wouldn't. I'd grab a bar of *soap* and wash myself back to land.

ROBINSON
(*Reassuringly.*) I'd take good care of him, Mum. (*Thinking.*) But better still . . . why don't *you* come, too? The owner's *still* looking for a cook and *you're* the best in the world.

MRS CRUSOE
(*Doubtfully.*) Oooh, I don't know. I've got very delicate skin, and all that salty sea air could dry it out.

BILLY
Not if you do what Queen Cleopatra of *Egypt* used to do. She bathed in *milk* ev'ry morning, to make her skin all smooth and *silky.*

MRS CRUSOE
(*Scornfully.*) Well I don't believe *that*, for a start.

BILLY
Why not?

MRS CRUSOE
She couldn't squeeze into the *bottle*. (*Brightening.*) Mind you . . . it'd be cheaper than going to *China*. And I've always wanted to visit neurotic places.

ROBINSON
So what's it going to be? Shall I *ask* the owner to take you on?

MRS CRUSOE
(*Deciding.*) Why not? I can celebrate my twenty-first birthday at sea.

MUSIC No. 6 (ROBINSON, MRS CRUSOE *and* BILLY)

(*As the song ends,* BILLY *and* MRS CRUSOE *exit down R.*)

ROBINSON
(*Happily.*) It'll be *wonderful*, all of us at sea together. (*Remembering.*) But I must find the owner and check he's not hired anyone else in the meantime. Then it's time to kiss Polly goodbye 'til I'm back in Hull, pockets filled with gold, and ready to plan our wedding. (*Exits R.*)

(*As he exits, the lights dim and* DAVY JONES *enters D.L. in a green light.*)

DAVY
(*Tiredly.*) Aagh, let it *rest*, yer dozy lot. Yer wasting breath by boo-ing.
Old Davy's heard *far* worse before, whilst *mischief* he's been brewing.
Yer protests count for *nothing* 'cos I learned *my* dirty tricks
From them as thinks 'em up each day . . . MP's in British Politics.
And if yer think they're not *that* bad, you've *really* lost the plot.
Like *me*, they're in it for *themselves*, and *lust* for all the cash you've got.
No matter you be Labour . . . Lib'ral . . . Tory . . . *or* U-Kips,

They'll steal your baby's *piggy-bank*. While all *I* do, is rob sunk *ships*.
(*Pleading.*) So let's be pals, and help me out. At Crusoe I must strike.
Do I drown him the harbour, or just *bash* him with a marlin-spike?

(*Enter* CORAL FAIRY *R., in a white spot.*)

FAIRY
(*Shocked.*) You wretched creature of the deep. How *dare* you try incite
Our audience to help you in your evil deeds tonight?
Young Robinson you *shall* not harm. I thought I'd made that clear.
And no assistance will you get from *any* person here.

DAVY
(*Snarls.*) I've warned yer *once*, I'll warn yer *twice*, you interfering sprite,
What e'r yer *say*, or try to *do*, I'll rid the world of *him* tonight.

FAIRY
(*Smiles.*) Brave words. But pray remember *this*. Pride goes before a fall.
And *your* pride . . . thanks to Robinson . . . shall have the greatest fall of all.

(*She exits R., and the white light goes out.*)

DAVY
(*To audience, smirking.*) Bah. When Davy sets his mind . . .
Ain't *no one* interferes.
'Cos if they *does* . . . I'm tellin' yer . . .
They go home sheddin' *tears*.
An' as fer all you O.A.P.s. Scouts, Brownies, Guides and Cubs . . .
More *jeers* . . . and in the Interval . . . I'll *dribble* in yer ice-cream tubs.

(*Laughs nastily and exits L. The green light goes out
and others return to normal. As they do so,* HALE *and*
HEARTY *enter up R., and move down C.*)

HEARTY
(*Worried.*) Ooooh, I don't know getting jobs on a *ship* was a good idea.
Them wooden decks get all slippery when they're wet, and we could fall
overboard.

HALE
(*Scornfully.*) You're not worried about *that*, are you? The First Mate
told us *exactly* what do do if somebody fell into the sea and looked like
drowning. You wait 'til their head pops out of the water, then grab 'em
by their hair, pull 'em into the lifeboat, wrap a warm blanket round 'em
and give 'em a tot of rum.

HEARTY
I know. I know. But I had a practice of my *own* after he'd gone, and it
didn't seem to work.

HALE
How do you mean?

HEARTY
Well . . . I got three of the other sailors to jump in so I could pretend
to rescue 'em. And when the *first* one popped up, I grabbed hold of his
hair, pulled him into the boat, wrapped a warm blanket round him and
gave him a tot of rum.

HALE
So what was wrong with *that?* You did exactly what he *said* you'd to do.

HEARTY
I know. I know. And when the *second* one popped up, I grabbed *his* hair,
pulled him into the boat, wrapped a warm blanket round him and gave
him a tot of rum. Just like the first one. (*Grimacing.*) But I couldn't *do* it
with the *third* feller.

HALE
Don't tell me you ran out of rum and warm blankets?

HEARTY
No. He was bald as a badger. So I pushed him back under and told him
not to come up again 'til he'd grown enough hair for me to grab.

HALE
(*Pushing him.*) Ooooh, you get *dafter*, you do. If brains were food, you'd
starve to death. (*Remembering.*) Here. And speaking of food . . . we'd
better start looking for a Ship's Cook, like we were told. We can't sail
halfway round the world without somebody doing *meals* for us.

HEARTY
(*Wryly.*) I'd do it *myself*, but that rotten Jamie Olive-drops was giving me
cooking lessons, and sacked me for burning something to cinders.

HALE
(*Curious.*) What was it?

HEARTY
The kitchen.

(HALE *beats* HEARTY *with his cap, as* POLLY *hurries in down L.*)

POLLY
(*Anxiously.*) Excuse me, but you haven't seen Robinson Crusoe, have you?

HALE
(*Blankly.*) Robinson *who*-so?

POLLY
Crusoe. I've been looking for him, *everywhere.*

HALE
(*Shaking his head.*) Sorry love. Never *heard* of him. (*Replaces his cap.*)

POLLY
(*Concerned.*) Oh, dear. And I've *got* to find him before his ship sails. (*She looks around anxiously.*)

HEARTY
(*Knowingly.*) Want to kiss him goodbye, eh?

POLLY
Oh, no. *No.* I've just heard the most awful *rumour.* The ship he's *sailing* on belongs to an awful old miser who never pays the crew a penny of what he's promised them. And the way he treats them is *horrible.*

HALE
(*Wide eyed.*) Horrible?

POLLY
Yes. Every Saturday night, everyone on board is given a free barrel of beer, and he insists they drink it straight away.

HALE
(*Impressed.*) Sounds good to *me.* What's horrible about *that?*

POLLY
Well, after they've *done* it . . . he locks the lavatory door, turns on the fire sprinklers, and watches everyone *panicking.*

HALE
(*Imagining the scene.*) Oo-er. I wouldn't like to be on a ship like *that.*

HEARTY
Me neither.

POLLY
Well if you *haven't* seen Robinson, I'd better keep *looking* for him. His ship sails any minute, now.

HALE
So does *ours*. And unless we fmd a cook, it looks like we'll have to *starve*. (*Thinking quickly as he replaces his hat.*) Here . . . I don't suppose you know how to cook, do you?

POLLY
Of course I do.

HEARTY
(*Eagerly.*) And can you make *fishcakes?*

POLLY
(*Surprised.*) I *suppose* so. But *why?*

HEARTY
Our boss's got a pet *kipper* . . . and tomorrow's its tenth birthday.

POLLY
(*Apologetically.*) I'm sorry. But I *really* can't stay any longer. I *have* to find Robinson before it's too late.

HALE
And what about *us?* We can't go back to *our* ship without a cook.

POLLY
(*Helpfully.*) You could try *advertising.*

HALE
Advertising? (Scornfully.) You must be joking. My sister tried that last year when she wanted to get *married*, so she advertised for a husband in the (*Local newspaper.*) and got *six hundred* replies.

POLLY
(*Amazed.*) Six hundred? From men who wanted to marry her?

HEARTY
No. From women saying "You can have *mine.*"

HALE

(*Glowering.*) And *anyway* . . . We haven't got *time* to run around *advertising.* We want somebody *now* . . . an' if *you* can boil an egg, I reckon you'll do for *us.* (*To* HEARTY.) Quick. Grab her before she escapes.

(*They grab hold of her.*)

POLLY

(*Startled.*) What are you doing? (*Struggles.*) Let *go* of me. Let *go.*

HALE

To the ship with her.

(*They hurry her U.R. as she struggles.*)

POLLY

(*Calling.*) Help! Help!

(*They exit U.R. as the lights quickly fade and the scene ends.*)

Scene Four: Below Deck on The Jellied Eel.

A lane scene depicting a corridor, inset with portholes. Full lighting. As the scene begins, a group of babes or juniors dressed as rats perform a short dance routine.

MUSIC No. 7 (BABES *or* JUNIORS)

(*As the dance ends,* SIR PERCY *enters L. scowling and clutching a rolled up scroll. They squeal in alarm and scurry off hastily, R.*)

SIR PERCY

(*Glowering after them.*) Blisterin' barnacles. There's almost as many rats on me ship, as there are running (*Local County Council*). (*Unrolls the scroll to reveal large holes in it.*) Look what they've done to me map. Got more holes in it than a Swiss cheese. Good job I *knows* where we're heading with all my gold and precious stones. (*Throws the scroll off L.*) Now where's this cook young Crusoe's found for me? If she's any good, we can weigh anchor and be out of sight afore anybody in the tax office knows it.

(*Enter* MRS CRUSOE *R., in a new, outrageous gown.*)

MRS CRUSOE

(*To audience.*) Do you like the frock, girls? (*Turns around to exhibit it.*) Yes. I *thought* you would. The women in the front row turned green with envy when I came on. (*To front row.*) Well, there's no need to be *jealous*, ladies. I got it from (*Names local dress shop*). *Yes.* I popped in to get something for the voyage, and the the manageress was ever so *helpful*. "Mrs Crusoe," she said. "How can I help *you*, this morning?" Well, I said, "I'd like to see something *cheap* in a summer frock." "In that case," she said, "try *that* rail over *there*. (*Indicates.*) And the mirror's on the left." (*Beams.*) Oh, and I must tell you. It's ever so hard-wearing. It'll last for *years*. And it's not surprising, really, 'cos you'll never guess what it's *made* of. (*Confidentially.*) The same material they use to make *sun blinds* for all the posh shops, like Clic and Marie Curie. (*Frowns.*) Mind you . . . the minute it starts getting *dark,* the hem rolls up to me neckline and shows me versatility.

SIR PERCY

(*Pointedly.*) A-hem. (*Glowering.*) Forgive my *curiosity*, madam . . . but who the shivering swordfish are *you?* And what are you doing aboard me *ship?*

MRS CRUSOE

(*To audience, excitedly.*) Oooh, I say. It's Simon Cow-bell. (*Or other.*) (*To him.*) Diphtheria Crusoe, your Hijesty. (*Curtsies.*) Domestic goddess . . . and this week's special offer. (*Flutters her eyelashes at him.*)

SIR PERCY

(*Amazed.*) You mean . . . you're the new *cook?*

MRS CRUSOE

Oh, yes. And I've already taken a sample lunch to your cabin, so you can see how *good* I am. (*Beams.*)

SIR PERCY

(*Pleased.*) Well, well, well. (*To audience.*) I like the old faggot, already. (*To her.*) And *what*, exactly, have you *made* me for lunch?

MRS CRUSOE

Well . . . I found a nice bit of *steak* in the ships freezer, so I thought you could have *that*, for a start.

SIR PERCY
(*Suspiciously.*) Well I hope you've cooked it *properly*. I like *my* steaks as tender as a mermaid's kiss.

MRS CRUSOE
Oh, you'll like *this* then. It'll *melt* in your *mouth*. I didn't have time to defrost it

SIR PERCY
(*Scowling.*) Bah.

MRS CRUSOE
(*Remembering.*) Here . . . and by the *way*. Is there a *lavvy* on this thing? I couldn't fmd one *anywhere* and I can't go sailing round the hemisphere if there's no lavvy.

SIR PERCY
(*Scowling.*) Of course there's a *lavvy*.

MRS CRUSOE
(*Mollified.*) Well that's all right, then. As long as you've not forgotten the *toilet rolls*.

SIR PERCY
(*Baffled.*) *Toilet* rolls?

MRS CRUSOE
(*Reasonably.*) Well, they don't *all* have 'em, you know. The last one I went into didn't have *anything*. Talk about *embarrassing*. I had to call to the woman in the next cubicle and ask if she'd any toilet roll in *hers*. "I *haven't*," she said. "There's nothing here at all." So I thought for a minute, then asked if she'd any *newspaper?*" "No," she said. "There's none of that *either*. I don't think there's *any* kind of paper in *this* place." "Well in that case," I said "Have you two five pound notes for a tenner?"

SIR PERCY
(*Taking a deep breath.*) So . . . Yer wants to be cook for *The Jellied Eel*, do yer?

MRS CRUSOE
I *do*. Yes. I *do*. (*Beaming.*) I can't *wait* to to get my first glimpse of foreign parts. Especially Mount Everest.

SIR PERCY
(*Incredulously.*) Mount *Everest?*

MRS CRUSOE
Oh, yes. I was talking to a fella in (*Local coffee shop.*) this morning,
and he said if I could only visit one place in my life, it had to be Mount
Everest. "Mind you," he said. "It's twenty-nine thousand feet high, so
try not to fall *off* it. But if you do . . . look to the left as you're dropping,
'cos the view's *amazing.*

SIR PERCY
(*Glowering.*) Yes. Well yer can forget about Mount Everest. We ain't
going anywhere near it. *We're* going somewhere *exotic*, where
faberlous perfumes an' *pungent spices* drifts past yer nostrils on warm
intoxicating breezes. (*Breathes it all in dreamily.*)

MRS CRUSOE
(*Surprised.*) Not (*Local Indian Restaurant.*)?

SIR PERCY
(*Snorting.*) Bah. Get down to the galley and start cooking something
cheap.

MRS CRUSOE
How about a Good King Wenceslas pizza?

SIR PERCY
(*Baffled.*) Good King Wenceslas *pizza?* What are they like?

MRS CRUSOE
Deep pan. Crisp. And even. (*Chortles and pushes him playfully.*) *I've*
waited years to use *that* one.

SIR PERCY
(*Snarling and lifting his stick.*) Yes. And *I've* waited years to use *this*.

> (*As he advances towards her, she reacts, turns and
> rushes off, R. With a yell of fury, he stomps after her. As
> they exit,* ROBINSON *enters L.*)

ROBINSON
(*Cheerfully.*) Just a few more minutes and we'll be on our way to . . .
well . . . wherever the sea-breeze takes us. (*Remembering.*) But *this*
time, I'll do my best not to get shipwrecked on a *desert island.* I still
don't know how I survived. All those years, with no one to talk to until
I met *Friday* . . . the best friend a man could ever have. (*Brightening.*)
Now here I am again . . . about to sail the Seven Seas, and *this* time with
Mother and Billy on board to share the adventure. (*Wistfully.*) If only

Polly were here, too, I'd be walking on clouds. (*Brightly.*) But I *know* she'll be there when we return . . . richer than shareholders in Starbucks . . . and everyone will see me walking down the aisle with the most beautiful girl in the world on my arm.

MUSIC No. 8 (ROBINSON)

> (*As the song ends,* BILLY *enters R. He wears an over-sized (or too small) sailor suit, a snorkel mask on his forehead, frogman's flippers, life-belt, and inflated arm bands.*)

BILLY
(*Calling unhappily.*) Hiya, kids.

> (*Audience response.*)

ROBINSON
(*Amused.*) What on earth are you doing in *that* lot?

BILLY
(*Miserably.*) Mum said I'd to be prepared, in case I fell overboard. According to *her*, I'd either get wet and catch a cold, or be swallowed by a *shark*.

ROBINSON
(*Sympathetically.*) I suppose she's just being *protective.*

BILLY
I know. But I *told* her there was nothing to worry about. I've got some life-saving words tattooed on me chest in big red letters.

ROBINSON
(*Puzzled.*) Life-saving *words?*

BILLY
Yes. They say "Gordon Brown was the best Prime Minister Britain's ever had." And even a *shark* won't swallow *that.*

ROBINSON
(*Amused.*) Oh, Billy. You *do* make me laugh.

BILLY
(*Dolefully.*) I wish I could make *meself* laugh. I'm really depressed, I am.

ROBINSON
(*Puzzled.*) But why? You *should* be on top of the world. We're about to set out on the adventure of a lifetime.

BILLY
I know. But I *always* get depressed when I see a *funeral.* And there was one down our street a few minutes ago.

ROBINSON
(*Surprised.*) Really? Who died?

BILLY
The man in the coffin. Mind you . . . the undertaker was ever so thoughtful. As soon as he heard the news, he went round and asked if she wanted her husband buried, embalmed, or cremated?

ROBINSON
And what did she *say?*

BILLY
Don't take chances. Do all three.

ROBINSON
(*Cheerfully.*) Well, I'm sure a few hours on board will cheer you up. By the time night falls, your lungs will be full of good sea air and we'll be well on our way to fame and fortune.

BILLY
Yes. But how will we know where we *are?*

ROBINSON
By working out the latitude and longitude, of course.

BILLY
(*Baffled.*) What's latitude and longitude?

ROBINSON
Well . . . *latitude* is the distance, measured in degrees, of a place between North or South of the equator. And *longitude* is the distance measured in degrees, of a place East or West of the Greenwich meridian.

BILLY
(*To audience.*) Ask a silly question . . .

ROBINSON
(*Patiently.*) I'll make it *simpler* for you. Supposing I ask you to meet me for dinner, at latitude sixteen degrees *North*, and longitude ten degrees, *East* . . . what would *that* tell you?

BILLY
That I wouldn't be getting any dinner.

ROBINSON
(*Laughing.*) Oh, Billy. We're *never* going to make a sailor of *you*. It's a good job we're not living in the *old* days. You had to know *everything* about ships, *then*.

BILLY
(*Defensively.*) I can tell port from starboard.

ROBINSON
(*Questioningly.*) Really? And how do you do *that?*

BILLY
I look at the label on the bottles.

ROBINSON
(*Amused.*) And what about hoisting your *halyards?* Do you think you could manage *that?*

BILLY
Not in *these* trousers.

ROBINSON
(*Amused.*) Well before we weigh anchor, I'd better show you around. It's not like being on land, you know. *Most* things have different names to the ones you're used to. For instance . . . a window's a *porthole* . . . the floor's a *deck*. The rooms are *cabins*, the beds are *hammocks*, the kitchen's a *galley*, the toilet's a *head*, and the dining room's a *mess*.

BILLY
(*Scowling.*) Well don't ask *me* to clean it up.

> (ROBINSON *shakes his head in disbelief and exits R.,*
> *followed by* BILLY. *As they do so, the lights dim rapidly*
> *and* DAVY JONES *enters L., in a green follow spot.*)

DAVY
(*To audience.*) In vain he dreams of wealth untold.

Of treasure chests, and bags of gold.
(*Gloating.*) For though he's young and passing brave,
Tonight he'll sleep in watery grave,
With *lobsters* chewing at his bones.
A victim of old Davy Jones. (*Chortles nastily.*)

(*Enter* FAIRY, *R., in a white follow spot.*)

FAIRY
(*Firmly.*) You've really gone too far, this time
So bid farewell to life of crime.
King Neptune orders, cease your plots
To scuttle ships, and ocean yachts.
Or by his Crown and Trident, he
Will banish you. *Immediately.*

DAVY
(*In mock fear.*) Oh, dear. I'm tremblin' in me boots.
(*Savagely.*) For Neptune, I don't give two hoots.
And very soon I'll make him see
The *real* king of the ocean's *me.*

FAIRY
(*Shocked.*) Such arrogance. You'd disobey
An order of our *king?*
In all the centuries I've lived,
I've never *heard* of such a thing.
Since time began, that kindly man
Upon our throne has sat.

DAVY
(*Sneering.*) Then tell him I'm *revolting.*

FAIRY
Oh . . . I think we *all* know *that.*

DAVY
Enough. I've things to *do.* The anchor's weighed. They're setting sail.
I've tidal waves to summon up . . . plus whirlpools . . . and a fearsome gale.
(*Smirks.*) The Jellied Eel will, like a stone, sink to the ocean bed.
And all on board will perish. Even *Crusoe* will be dead.
As for the *treasure* stowed on board, I'll offer grateful thanks . . .
While on the surface, naught remains but scattered oaken planks.

(*Laughs harshly and exits L. The green light goes out.*)

FAIRY
(*To audience.*) Don't worry. Even though it seems
The shipping forecast's grim.
Young Robinson, with *me* to help,
Will be an *easy* match for *him*.
So at old Davy's wicked threats,
Just roll your eyes and grin . . .
No matter how he rants and raves,
Against Crusoe, he'll never win.

> (*She waves her wand and exits R., the white light going
> out as the scene ends in a blackout.*)

Scene Five: The Deck of The Jellied Eel.

*Full lighting. The deck of a great galleon, looking towards the bow. A
pale blue backdrop suggests the sky. A raised section C.B. supports the
main mast and behind it, the ship's wheel. Beneath this section, a door
leads to below deck, and from opposite sides of the section, short flights
of steps lead down to the main deck. Ships rails and perhaps cannons,
L. and R.*

When the scene begins, it is bright and sunny. A HELMSMAN *is at the
wheel, back to the audience. Other* CREW, *male and female, in ragged
and shabby nautical dress, are singing and dancing.*

MUSIC No. 9 (CREW)

*At the end of the song, all fall back into small groups, chatting silently
and with some animation.* HALE *and* HEARTY *enter from below deck, and
move down C.F.*

HEARTY
Ooooh, thank goodness we're under way. She didn't want to come *with*
us, that new cook. Did she?

HALE
(*Snorting.*) Lot of fuss about nothing, if you ask me. Wait "til she sees
those tropical islands covered in coconut palms and surrounded by blue
sea and golden sand. She'll be begging us to *leave* her there. It'd cost her
a *fortune* if she went to a Travel Agent.

HEARTY
I know. But she wouldn't *do* that, would she? Go to a Travel Agent.

HALE
(*Blankly.*) Why not?

HEARTY
Well *I* went to a Travel Agent last year, and they sent me to *Africa.*

HALE
(*Impressed.*) Africa? Ooooh, I've *always* wanted to go to *Africa.*
(*Dreamily.*) Eli-potomus . . . rhino-mongeese . . . Gira-whatsits.
(*Eagerly.*) Where did you stay?

HEARTY
The Ripoff Hotel . . . and it was right at the edge of the *Sahara desert.*
Well, I couldn't find it *anywhere* . . . so I phoned 'em up and asked
where it was. "Oh, you can't miss us," the manager said. "We're just a
stone's throw from the airport." "Yes," I said, "But how will I recognize
it?" "Easy," he said, "The windows are all smashed."

HALE
Well you can't blame the Travel Agent for *that.*

HEARTY
No. But I can blame him for the *other* thing. He didn't give me a *map*
and I got lost in the desert. Ooooh, it wasn't half *hot,* and I didn't have
anything to drink for three whole days.

HALE
(*Incredulously.*) Three *days?*

HEARTY
(*Unhappily.*) Yes. And I was so thirsty, I thought I was going to *die.*

HALE
(*Interested.*) So what did you *do?*

HEARTY
Well . . . Just as I fell over, I spotted a tent in the distance, and managed
to crawl to it.

HALE
So whoever *owned* it, saved your life?

HEARTY
No. He said he'd nothing to drink at all, and only sold *ties.* But if I was

interested, he could sell me a red silk one with pyramids, mosquitoes and crocodiles all over it. "Are you crackers?" I said. "I don't want a *tie*. I'm dying of *thirst*. I want a glass of *water*." "Oh," he said. "If it's water you want, there's another tent in five miles, where all they *sell* is water." (*With great drama*.) So off I went again . . . crawling over the sand, slowly frying to death in the blazing, scorching, sun, 'til I came to the other tent which had a sign over the opening saying "All the ice-cold water you can drink."

HALE
So you crawled inside?

HEARTY
Yes. And the fella who owned the place, picked me up and threw me out again.

HALE
(*Baffled*.) What for?

HEARTY
He said I couldn't go in without wearing a tie.

> (HALE *snatches off his hat and beats* HEARTY *with it. Enter* SIR PERCY *from below, fuming. He is followed by an angry looking* POLLY.)

SIR PERCY
(*Loudly and aggressively*.) Shiver me timbers and call me Jessie. Who brought *this* dainty damsel on board me ship?

> (*As they move down C.F., the crew turn to pay attention and* HALE *and* HEARTY *move quickly R*.)

POLLY
(*Indicating them*.) They're the ones. They kidnapped me on shore and locked me up inside that awful cabin.

> (HALE *and* HEARTY *back further away*.)

HALE
It was only 'til we *sailed* . . . and we couldn't keep you in *our* cabin.

HEARTY
No. It's freezing cold . . . and every time you close the door, the little light goes out.

HALE
And besides . . . we've never been to sea before, and all we'd got in there
was a bottle of rum, some ship's biscuits that are hard enough to break
your teeth on, and half a dozen teensy-weensy mice. (*Pretends to be a
mouse.*)

SIR PERCY
(*Glowering.*) *Mice?*

HEARTY
(*Defensively.*) Well *something's* got to eat the biscuits.

(CREW *look amused.*)

POLLY
(*Firmly.*) I demand to be taken back at once.

SIR PERCY
(*Amazed.*) Yer must be joking. We're heading for the High Seas with a
precious cargo, afore we can be stopped.

(*All the* CREW *agree.*)

POLLY
(*Blankly.*) Precious cargo?

SIR PERCY
(*Proudly.*) Stashed below decks, safe from prying eyes and nestling
inside a gigantic, impregnable chest.

(*Enter* MRS CRUSOE, *from below, in another new outfit.*)

MRS CRUSOE
(*Beaming.*) Someone mention *me?* (*Caresses her bust.*)

POLLY
(*Surprised.*) Mrs Crusoe. What are *you* doing here? Don't say you've
been kidnapped, too?

MRS CRUSO
(*Moving down C. F.*) Not *lately*. Mind you . . . I'd a narrow escape *last*
week. I saw this fella walking down the street carrying two chickens, a
baby pig, a big bucket and an anvil. "Here," I said, "What are you doing
with *that* lot?" "Well," he said, "I'm a farmer, and my tractor's broken
down, so I'm having to *carry* everything home. You wouldn't like to

give me a hand, would you?" "No fear," I said. "I've got my best frock on, and I don't want to get it dirty. And besides . . . how do I know you won't wait 'til we're somewhere secluded, then suddenly pounce on me and start kissing and cuddling?" "Don't be daft," he said. "How could I do *that?* I'm carrying a bucket, a baby pig, two chickens and an anvil." "Yes," I said" But if you put the pig on the ground, put the bucket over it and weighed it down with the anvil . . . *I* could hold the chickens."

(CREW *are amused.*)

POLLY
But you still haven't explained what you're doing here?

MRS CRUSOE
Trying to cook the dinner for tonight. But I'm having a bit of trouble with the oven. It's one of those new fangled *microwave* things and I've never used one before, so it's taking *ages* to pre-heat it. I've used ten boxes of matches already.

HALE
(*Protesting.*) Hang on a minute. Hang on. You can't be the ship's cook. We brought *her* (*Indicates* POLLY.) here, to do that job.

HEARTY
Yes. Everybody's fed up with *rabbit.* Ever since they landed in Hull, they'd had nothing to eat but rabbit. Rabbit *pie,* rabbit *stew,* rabbit *casserole*, rabbit *soup,* rabbit *salad.* Whenever they heard a dog bark, they hid down the nearest hole.

MRS CRUSOE
Well you needn't worry about rabbits. I'm doing something really *special* for tonight. (*Coyly.*) Sprout and Ginger Casserole, with Peppermint toothpaste sauce.

SIR PERCY
(*Glowering.*) Sounds *disgusting.*

(*The others agree.*)

MRS CRUSOE
Yes . . . but think of the advantages. You can have your dinner and brush your teeth at the same time. (*To audience.*) Who needs dentists, when I'm around? (*Beams.*)

HEARTY
I went to a dentist once . . . but never again. Instead of having a chair that went up and down, *his* went backwards and forwards. It was real tight fit as well, and he was ever so rude to me.

HALE
Why? What did he say?

HEARTY
(*Embarrassed.*) Get out of the filing cabinet, you fathead.

POLLY
(*Indignantly.*) Well never mind all that. What I want to know is how I'm going to get back to *land.* I have to find Robinson and warn him about the danger he's in.

(*All look surprised.*)

SIR PERCY
Danger?

POLLY
He's about to set sail on a ship full of crooks, thieves, swindlers, cheaters, and every *other* kind of villain.

SIR PERCY
(*Scowling.*) I didn't know the *Houses of Parliament* had their own ship.

MRS CRUSOE
(*To* POLLY, *beaming.*) Well you don't have to worry, dear. He's doing nothing of the kind. He's here on this ship with me and Billy. (*Glances off R.*) Look. Here he comes now.

(*Enter* ROBINSON, *down R.*)

POLLY
Robinson! (*Hurries to him.*)

ROBINSON
(*Surprised.*) Polly! I thought you were miles away. (*Takes her hands.*)

POLLY
And *I* thought I'd never *see* you again.

ROBINSON
(*Curious.*) But what are you *doing* here?

POLLY
It doesn't matter now. Not now I know that you're safe.

ROBINSON
(*Amused.*) Well, of course I'm safe. We *all* are. This is the finest ship
that's ever sailed. (*Anxiously.*) But how are we going to get you back to
land? We're miles from Hull, now.

SIR PERCY
And we ain't goin' back for nobody. But I can find her a job on board if
she don't mind earning her keep.

MRS CRUSOE
She can help *me* in the *kitchen*.

SIR PERCY
Good idea. And as fer the rest of yer . . . there's work to be done, so get
doing it or yer'll feel me stick about yer shoulders.

> (*Everyone but the* HELMSMAN, ROBINSON *and* POLLY *exit
> variously, in haste.*)

ROBINSON
(*Happily.*) Oh, Polly. I can't *believe* you're sailing with me. It's
something I've always dreamed of. The two of us together, and the
whole world waiting to be explored. (*Excitedly.*) Have you ever seen a
real coconut palm? Or a turtle? Or even a *dolphin?*

POLLY
(*Laughing.*) I'm afraid not. But I don't even care, as long as I'm with *you*.

MUSIC No. 9 (ROBINSON *and* POLLY.)

> (*After the song, they exit R. As they do so,* BILLY *enters
> from below, carrying two plastic buckets loaded with
> assorted rubbish (see production notes). He now wears
> a brighter version of a male crew member's costume,
> and has a big bright coloured plastic clothes-peg on his
> nose.*)

BILLY
(*Wearily.*) Hiya, kids. (*Moves down C.F., puts the buckets down and
removes the clothes-peg.*) Oooh. Talk about rotten jobs. I've had to
collect all this rubbish from below deck, and it doesn't half pong. (*Looks
at the buckets.*) Fish *heads*, rotten *apples*, mouldy bread and sweaty

socks. They're all in there. And *maggots*. You've never *seen* such big maggots. (*Plaintively.*) What am I going to *do* with it all? Sir Percy said if he finds one speck of dirt on his nice clean deck, there's going to be *trouble*. (*He suddenly brightens.*) Here. I know. You're all friends of mine, aren't you? If I throw it to *you*, you could take it home and put it in your wheelie bins. It'd only be a handful each, and you can put it in your pockets or your handbags 'til we've finished. (*Happily.*) Thanks, mates. (*Puts the peg back on his nose, picks up a bucket and prepares to throw the contents into the audience.*)

> (*Enter* HALE *and* HEARTY *R.* HEARTY *carries a sweeping brush.*)

HALE
(*Calling.*) Hey. Hey. What do you think you're *doing?*

> (BILLY *halts, puts down the bucket and removes the peg.*)

BILLY
I'm getting rid of this rubbish and my mates in the audience are going to take it home for me.

HALE
(*Peers into the bucket, and recoils.*) Blimey. *They're* a brave lot.

HEARTY
(*Pulling a face.*) Smells like school dinners. (*Backs away.*)

BILLY
(*Grimacing.*) I *know*. And I've *soaked* it with loads and loads of *fragrance.*

HEARTY
(*Puzzled.*) What's *fragrance?*

HALE
(*Tiredly.*) It's a posh name for *perfume*, you ignorosopus. You use it to cover up even *worse* smells. (*To* BILLY.) And *they're* going to take it away for you? (*Indicates audience.*)

BILLY
(*Happily.*) Yes.

HALE
(*Looking into the audience.*) And I thought *he* (*Indicates* HEARTY.) was crackers. (*To* BILLY.) We'll give you a hand, then. I'm starting to

feel poorly already. (*He crosses* BILLY *and picks up the second bucket warily.*) Sooner we get rid of it, the better. (*Faces audience and prepares to throw the contents.*) Who wants it first?

BILLY
(*Picking up his own bucket.*) Try the woman in the front row. She's got a big *handbag.* You'll get *lots* in there.

HALE
(*To "victim".*) All right, missis. Open it up wide. Don't want to get it on your frock, do we?

> (BILLY *and* HALE *swing the buckets back to toss the contents.*)

HEARTY
(*Hastily.*) Just a minute. Just a minute.

> (*They pause.*)

You can't throw that into the *audience.* There's not enough to go *round.* If you're not careful, you'll have 'em *fighting* for it and you don't want 'em going home with black eyes and broken noses.

BILLY
(*To* HALE.) He's right. He's right. I don't want anybody going home upset 'cos they didn't get a maggot or a fish head. We'll throw it over the side.

> (*Moves R., tosses the rubbish overboard, then turns back to the others, beaming.*)

There. All gone.

> (*The rubbish comes flying back and covers him.*)

Ahhhhhhhh.

> (*Brushes it off frantically as others laugh.*)

HALE
(*Smugly.*) It's easy to see *you* know nothing about ships. You threw it the wrong side, didn't you? You're supposed to check which way the wind's blowing, first. Watch *me.* (*Licks his finger and holds it up.*) Right. It's blowing from that direction, (*Indicates L.*), so you throw it over there.

> (*As* BILLY *disgustedly takes the brush from* HEARTY *and*

begins to sweep up the returned rubbish, HALE *moves L. and tosses the contents of the bucket off L., then turns to face the others.*)

There you are, see? Gone without trace . . .

(*The rubbish comes flying back and covers him.*)

Ahhhhhhhhh . . .

(*Brushes it off frantically as others laugh.*)

BILLY
(*Worried.*) Oh, look at all the *mess.* If Sir Percy sees this, he'll go crackers. (*Begins frantically sweeping the rubbish into a heap.*)

HEARTY
(*Looking off L.*) Oooh. Look out. He's coming *now.*

HALE
(*Panicking.*) Quick, quick Throw everything over the side.

(*They frantically gather up all the rubbish, including the buckets and brush, and toss them over the side R., then all scuttle L. and stand to attention as* SIR PERCY *enters down L. and passing them, moves C.*)

SIR PERCY
(*Glowering.*) Everything nice and ship-shape, maties?

TOGETHER
Everything nice and ship-shape. (*They salute him.*)

(*An enormous amount of rubbish is thrown back on L., which swamps them and* SIR PERCY, *who howls with fury, and brandishes his stick, With yells of fear, the trio race upstage and exit below deck, with* SIR PERCY *in furious pursuit. As they all vanish, the lights dim and* DAVY JONES *enters down L. in a green light.*)

DAVY
(*Triumphantly.*) Come thunder, lightning, rain and gale.
Reduce to tatters, ev'ry sail.
Come mighty waves to pound and blast,
Transform to *splinters*, ev'ry mast.

(The lights begin to flicker and thunder sounds.)

Come ev'ry hazard I desire . . .
Thick *fog*. Black *ice*. St. Elmo's Fire.
Come creatures from the ocean deep
That dwell in darkness, swim or creep.
Destroy all those who'd thwart my plan
To own more gold than *any* man.

(Lights flicker madly, with louder thunder.)

Come whirlpools of gigantic size
And seize this vessel as my prize.
So all its cargo . . . gold and stones . . .
Can tumble down to Davy Jones. *(Cackles with laughter and exits L.)*

> *(More loud thunder sounds, lightning flashes as a terrible storm breaks. Various CREW stagger onto the deck, being thrown from side to side and shouting in fright. The HELMSMAN battles with the wheel. ROBINSON and POLLY enter R. MRS CRUSOE appears C. All are staggering side to side as the ship rolls and tosses.)*

MRS CRUSOE
(Alarmed.) What's happening? *(Staggers.)*

ROBINSON
(Staggering.) It's the ship. I think it's sinking.

POLLY
(Calling.) Find a lifeboat. *(Staggers.)*

MRS CRUSOE
Never mind a lifeboat. Find me a *lifeguard. (To audience.)* I used to love *Baywatch. (Lurches sideways with a shriek of fear.)*

> *(SIR PERCY staggers on, followed by BILLY, HALE and HEARTY. All are panicking.)*

SIR PERCY
(Calling loudly.) Abandon ship. Abandon ship.

> *(All wail with fear as they stumble side to side, the storm gets worse, and the CURTAIN CLOSES for the Interval.)*

ACT TWO

Scene One: The Island of Migrainia.

A full set. The tropical island of Migrainia. Backdrop depicts a view of the calm sea and sandy beach, with tropical palm trees. Other palms mask entrances and exits L. and R. On the floor, C.F. is a shoe inner-sole. When the scene begins, it is daylight, and the ISLANDERS *who are dressed in nationalistic costumes of several countries and various periods in time, are singing and dancing.* ISLANDERS 3 & 4 *are similarly dressed, as both are from the same country and time.*

MUSIC No. 10

At the end of the song, all fall back into small groups as CODINE, *the Court Chamberlain, enters up L., and moves down C.F. He is a small man dressed in the apparel of an Ancient Egyptian, Mayan, or Greek, who seems bowed down with worry, and carries a tall staff of office. This is about shoulder height, bone coloured. and tapers to a point. It is hung with several decorative ribbons.*

ALL
Good Morning, Lord Chamberlain Codine. (*All bow politely.*)

CODINE
(*Wearily.*) What's good about it? That terrible stonn kept me wide awake all night. I suppose *Davy Jones* is back again?

1ST ISLANDER
Not that we *know* of, Your Lordship. Nobody's *seen* him.

2ND ISLANDER
That's why we were *celebrating*. It must have been just an *ordinary* storm.

CODINE
(*Shaking his head.*) That was no ordinary storm, young lady / man. It's the worst I've seen in over two thousand years.

3RD ISLANDER
(*Surprised.*) Two thousand *years?*

CODINE (*Tiredly.*)
Oh, *yes*. That's how long I've *been* marooned on this island.

4TH ISLANDER
(*Amused.*) But that's *impossible*. No one lives that *long*.

CODINE
They *do* on Migrainia. And *some* here are even *older*.

(*Others agree.*)

It's part of a magic spell, you see? Cast by Davy Jones. If you're
shipwrecked *here*, you've to stay 'til the end of your life. And
unfortunately, if you drink from the Fountain of Youth . . . which is the
only water on the island . . . you never age at all.

3RD ISLANDER
(*Stunned.*) But that means we could be here *forever*.

CODINE
Unless someone breaks the spell.

(*All nod unhappily.*)

4TH ISLANDER
(*Protesting.*) But no one told us this when we arrived last week.

CODINE
Last *week*? No, no, dear friends. You've been here *much* longer than
that. Fifty years, at least. Time never passes, you see? That's why
you can't remember clearly. If I didn't keep a diary of everything that
happens here, even *I'd* forget.

3RD ISLANDER
(*Curious.*) But what's Davy Jones got to do with it? He isn't *real*.
Everyone knows that. He's just a sailor's *legend*. Like sea-serpents and
mermaids.

(DAVY *enters down L., in a green light. All react.*)

DAVY
(*Harshly.*) Foolish mortal, not to fear the bile of he who *keeps* you here.
Old Davy *ain't* no sailor myth . . . I'm real as *any* kin or kith. (*Leers.*)
And on this isle I vow you'll stay, 'til Time itself has passed away.

CODINE
(*Nervously.*) You've told us that *before*, Mr Jones, but never said *why*.

DAVY
(*Snarling.*) 'Cos male or female . . . old or young . . .
No mortal ever holds their tongue.
Of *gossip*, no one seems to tire,
And spreads it like a forest fire.
It's whispered, *now* . . . but what comes next?
They'll invent *E-mails, Twitter, Text.*
If *one* escaped, they'd scream and shout
And Davy's secret would be out.
For near this isle, for years I've stored
The finest of my rescued hoard.
Diamonds, emeralds, pearls divine,
Silver. Gold. And all is *mine.* (*Laughs in triumph.*)

(FAIRY *enters R. in a white light.*)

FAIRY
(*Smiling.*) But not for long. As I foretold,
You'll *lose* your precious stones and gold.
Young Robinson will break your spell
And free all those who here do dwell.

(ISLANDERS *stare in astonishment and converse silently with each other.*)

DAVY
(*Sneering.*) You're out of touch, dear. Crusoe's *dead,*
And rests upon the ocean bed
With all the others of his kind.

FAIRY
Not so. As shortly you will find.
By mighty Neptune's own command
I brought all safely here, to land.

(DAVY *reacts in shock.*)

And though you strive with all your might,
Young Crusoe's *sure* to win the fight

DAVY
(*Angrily.*) Be silent, interfering fay.
I'll pay no heed to what *you* say.
And as for Crusoe, *mortal* born,
I've nothing but the deepest scorn.

FAIRY
Then fare-thee-well. The gauntlet's thrown.
We'll *see* who gains the victor's throne. (*She exits R.*)

(*The white light goes out.*)

DAVY
(*To audience, glowering.*) Poor deluded coral sprite . . .
She thinks I'm going to *lose* this fight
(*Taps his nose.*) But Davy knows a trick or two
And 'ere's what I intends to do.
(*In conspiratorial tones.*) I'll lay a most ingenious trap,
To snare this young North Country chap.
Then when he's fast, as fast can be,
Dispatch him, deep below the sea. (*Laughs nastily and exits L.*)

(*The green light goes out* CODINE *and the* ISLANDERS *become more animated.*)

CODINE
Quick We must tell the Queen that Davy Jones is back, then find this Robinson Crusoe fellow and *warn* him he's in danger.

(*All agree and quicldy exit variously.* HALE *and* HEARTY *stagger on up R. They are wearing ragged versions of their earlier outfits, and are carrying a huge, padlocked treasure chest. This should have small concealed wheels or sliders for later use. They cross to up C., with great effort.*)

HALE
(*Gasping.*) Oooooh. Wait a minute. Wait a minute. Let's have a rest.

(*They deposit the chest up C.*)

(*Relieved.*) Thank goodness for that. It must weigh a ton. I wonder what's inside it? (*Wanders down C.F.*)

HEARTY
(*Following.*) I hope it's something useful . . . like tins of food. We don't want to *starve* to death, do we?

HALE
(*Amused.*) You must be joking. Nobody starves to death in *this* place.
(*Waving his arms expansively.*) This is *America.*

HEARTY
(*Surprised.*) Is it? (*Looks round curiously.*)

HALE
Of *course* it is. Didn't you see that great big *statue* when we dragged ourselves out of the water? (*Dreamily.*) Holding a light above its head to welcome us to a new country. (*Strikes a similar pose.*)

HEARTY
(*Wide-eyed.*) Who is it? Florence Nightie-light?

HALE
(*Annoyed.*) No, it's *not* Florence Nightie-light. It's nothing *like* Florence Nightie-light. (*Proudly.*) It's the Statue of *Liberace.* (*Gleefully.*) Oh, we're going to have a *marvellous* time here, I can tell you. It'll be KFC, Big Macs and Coca Cola every day of the week.

HEARTY
(*Doubtfully.*) I don't know. According to my big brother, there's nothing in America but Red Indians and Buffalo.

HALE
No, no. Red Indians and *Bison*.

HEARTY
(*Shaking his head.*) Buffalo, *he* said.

HALE
(*Pompously.*) Then he got it *wrong.* And besides . . . there's hardly any difference between a bison and a buffalo.

HEARTY
Yes there *is*. You can't wash your hands in a buffalo.

>   (HALE *takes off his hat and beats Hearty before*
>   *replacing it.*)

(*Sourly.*) I think you missed a bit.

>   (HALE *snatches off his hat and lashes* HEARTY *with it*
>   *twice more before replacing it again.*)

HALE
(*Grumbling.*) You get *worse*, you do. (*Mockingly.*) My big brother says there's nothing in America. (*Nastily.*) You haven't even *got* a brother.

HEARTY

(*Indignantly.*) Yes, I have. I've got a *big* brother *and* a little brother. One's a University Graduate, and the other's out of work, as well.

HALE

(*Suddenly remembering.*) Here . . . And speaking of work . . . We still don't know what's inside that chest we found in the sea.

> (*They hurry back upstage and stare at it.*)

Look at the *size* of it. If only we had the key.

HEARTY

We wouldn't *need* a key if my grandad was here. He could open *locks* with his eyes shut. But look at him *now.* Ninety-three years old and been stuck on an island for the last fifty years.

HALE

(*Surprised.*) You mean *he's* shipwrecked, too?

HEARTY

No. He's in jail on the Isle of Wight.

HALE

(*Dismissively.*) Well never mind *that.* Whatever's in this chest could change our whole lives. We'll carry it to the foot of the cliffs over there (*Indicates off L.*) and open it with a rock.

HEARTY

(*Eagerly.*) And what if it's full of money?

HALE

Simple. We'll go half and half. *I'll* take the money and *you* can have the chest. (*Chortles.*) No. I'm only joking. Whatever's inside it, we split down the middle. Because we're mates, we are, and when you're mates, you share and share alike. Right?

HEARTY

(*Brightly.*) Right.

MUSIC No. 11 (HALE and HEARTY)

(*After the song, they pick up the chest and stagger off
L. As they vanish from view,* BILLY *enters R. He wears
a very ragged version of his last costume and looks
shattered.*)

BILLY
(*Calling weakly.*) Hiya, kids, Ooooooh. What a night. Nobody told me
we had a box full of yo-yos on board . . . and the ship sank twenty-
five times. And look at me *clothes.* (*Indicates them.*) I'm all tags and
ratters. It's a good job me mum can't see me. She'd go crackers. When I
was little, she used to make me put a clean pair of *socks* on every day. I
mean . . . how daft can you get? A clean pair of socks, every *day.* After
a *week*, I couldn't get my *shoes* on. (*Looks round.*) I wonder where I
am? I should have asked that *pigeon*, shouldn't I? The one who offered
to *help* me. I told you about *him*, didn't I? (*Audience response.*) No? Oh,
well . . . There I was, splashing about in the water and just going down
for the third time . . . when suddenly . . . this little tiny pigeon came out
of nowhere pulling a *surfboard.* "Grab hold of it," he shouted "and I'll
tow you to safety." (*Pulls a face.*) But I couldn't *do* it. They'd all laugh if
they knew I was pigeon-towed.

(*Enter* ROBINSON *and* POLLY, *R. equally bedraggled.*)

ROBINSON
(*Relieved.*) Billy. (*Hurries to him.*) Thank goodness you're safe. You're
not hurt, are you?

BILLY
No. But just as I got to land, I got stinged on the leg by a great big
jellyfish.

ROBINSON
(*Dismayed.*) Oh, no. *Some* of them are very poisonous. (*Brightening.*)
But luckily, I know lots of plants that can be used to take the pain away,
so wait here and I'll get you something to *put* on it.

BILLY
(*To audience.*) And folks think *I'm* daft. (*To* ROBINSON.) It'll be miles
away by now.

(ROBINSON *reacts.*)

POLLY
(*Glancing around.*) But what about everyone *else?* Have any of *them*
survived?

BILLY
I don't know. I haven't *seen* anyone else.

ROBINSON
(*Dismayed.*) Not even *mother?*

POLLY
(*Reassuringly.*) She *could* be on the *other* side of the island.

BILLY
'Course she could. She's a *champion* swimmer, our mum is. (*Proudly.*) I remember her diving off the top of the cliffs at Scarborough once, to save David Beckham (*Or other male personality.*) from drowning.

POLLY
(*Wide-eyed.*) Really?

BILLY
(*Smugly.*) Oh, *yes. And* knocked out six *other* women who were trying to get to him first . . .

ROBINSON
Well it's no use just *hoping* she's safe. We'd better go *look* for her.

BILLY
(*Smugly.*) Leave it to *me.* I'm real good at finding lost things. I bought a big chest of drawers, once, at a car boot sale in (*Local area*).

ROBINSON
(*Baffled.*) What's that got to do with it?

BILLY
Well, it was all locked up, and nobody had a key, so when I got it home, I forced one of the drawers open, and found it was packed full of people who hadn't seen daylight for *years* . . .

POLLY
What?

BILLY
Yes. It was a missing persons bureau. (*Chortles.*)

ROBINSON
(*Annoyed.*) Can't you be *serious* for once, Billy? Mother could be in terrible *danger,* and all *you're* doing is telling stupid jokes.

BILLY

(*Squirming.*) Well . . . I didn't want to come on *this* voyage. I only did it for something to do. (*Unhappily.*) I'd just failed the audition for a new talent show on television.

ROBINSON

(*Surprised.*) Doing *what?*

BILLY

Stand up comedy. But when I'd *finished*, the judges said I'd better try something else. If all I could do was tell *jokes*, people would laugh at me.

POLLY

(*Helplessly.*) If only we knew where to search (*Glances around.*)

ROBINSON

(*Looking down and pointing.*) Look.

BILLY

(*Awed.*) A *footstep.* (*Picks up the inner-sole and displays it.*)

ROBINSON

Well, at least we now know *something.* We're not *alone* on the island. Someone else must have survived. Let's hope it's mother. (To BILLY) You go *that* way, (*Indicates L.*) we'll go *this* (*Indicates R.*), and see who we can find.

> (*They quickly exit down L. and R. As they do so,* SIR
> PERCY *totters on up R. He too is in a battered condition.*)

SIR PERCY

(*Dazed.*) Stap me vittals, and souse me trunnions. I've never seen a storm like it And now me *ship's* gone. Not to mention me lovely *treasure.* (*Sobs, then brightens.*) Unless it's been washed *ashore.* (*Hurries down C F, to speak to the audience.*) Ahoy, there, shipmates. You ain't seen no sign of Sir Percy's treasure chest, have yer? (*Persuasively.*) There's a nice shiny *penny* for the first one as spots it. (*Scowling.*) An' a thick ear if yer tries to open it with yer grubby fingers. (*All sweetness and light again.*) All you has to do, is let me know if yer come across a battered old wreck on the beach.

> (*Enter* MRS CRUSOE *up R., in a fantastic new costume.*)

MRS CRUSOE
(*Beaming.*) Here, I *am*, dear. Here, I *am*. (*Moves down to join him.*)

SIR PERCY
(*Aside.*) Blast. It's the ugly old faggot what did the ship's cooking.

MRS CRUSOE
(*Relieved.*) Oooh, thank goodness I've found you. (*Glances behind her.*) I've just been followed. By a feller in a grass skirt and feathers.

SIR PERCY
Are you sure it weren't an ostrich?

MRS CRUSOE
Oh, no. It was a feller, all right. He followed me all along the beach, up the cliff, under the waterfall, and through the jungle. I walked ever so slow, but he wouldn't catch up. (*Looks off R. again.*)

SIR PERCY
(*Sourly.*) I'm not surprised. (*Aside.*) So. There's somebody *else* on the island? And probably after me treasure chest. Well I'll soon put a stop to *that*. (*To* MRS CRUSOE.) He . . . er . . . he weren't *carrying* anything, were he? Like a *metal detector*, fer instance?

MRS CRUSOE
(*Remembering.*) Well it's funny you should *say* that . . . because he *was* carrying something. A *pencil* . . . and a sheet of very thin *paper*.

SIR PERCY
(*Frowning.*) What were he doing with *them?*

MRS CRUSOE
Trying to trace survivors (*Chortles and pushes him playfully.*)

(*He staggers sideways.*)

Oooh. And that reminds me. I've not seen anybody *else* from the shipwreck, yet. Have you?

SIR PERCY
(*Snarling.*) No, I ain't. And I'm not wastin' time *looking* for 'em. I'm keeping me weather eye out for somethin' *far* more important.

MRS CRUSOE
(*Indignantly.*) I *beg* your puddin'. *Nothing's* more important than finding my lovely boys.

SIR PERCY
(*Caustically.*) And what makes *them* so important?

MRS CRUSOE
Well . . . they're both *famous*, aren't they? Billy invented the world's first ejection seat for helicopters. And Robinson invented the four day week.

SIR PERCY
Four day week?

MRS CRUSOE
Yes. All his work was done by *Friday*.

> (*She chortles, and again pushes* SIR PERCY *playfully. He staggers sideways and off L. There is a great crash.*)

(*To audience, delightedly.*) You've been waiting for that one all night, haven't you? Oh, he likes a giggle, old Sir Percival. I could tell that the minute I met him. And talk about romantic. He was banging on my cabin door for nearly an hour last night. But I wouldn't open it. No, fear. I didn't want to let him out.

> (SIR PERCY *re-enters, dazedly, holding his head and clutching a large coconut.*)

SIR PERCY
(*Glowering.*) Flea-bitten old bandicoot. You've gone and cracked me skull. Got a headache now like nobody's business.

MRS CRUSOE
(*To audience, dryly.*) Typical feller. Always blames somebody else. (*To him.*) You know what *your* trouble is, don't you? You don't eat the right *foods*. Tell me what your *favourite* is.

SIR PERCY
(*Sarcastically.*) Stewed snooker balls. (*Throws the coconut off L.*)

MRS CRUSOE
(*Puzzled.*) Snooker balls?

SIR PERCY
(*Savagely.*) Yes. I has two reds fer *breakfast*, Three yellows and a black fer *lunch*. Four pinks and a white fer *dinner* and six browns fer *supper*. (*Glares at her.*) Satisfied?

MRS CRUSOE
Well it's no wonder you've got a headache, then. You're not eating enough *greens*. But never mind. I'll cook us a nice lunch, then we can have a look round and see if we can fmd the others.

SIR PERCY
(*Glowering.*) How can yer cook *lunch* if the galley's at the bottom of the sea?

MRS CRUSOE
Well you don't have to have a *kitchen* to cook in. When I was in the Brownies, I learned how to make a fire out of doors.

SIR PERCY
(*Suspiciously.*) And where're yer going to find doors on *this* island? Anyways . . . we ain't got *time* fer eating. We've no time fer *anything* 'til I'm holding me lovely treasure again.

MRS CRUSOE
(*Indignantly.*) You haven't held me the *first* time, yet. (*Coyly.*) Mind you . . . I wouldn't struggle if you tried to give me a little kiss while nobody's looking. (*Puckers her lips at him.*)

SIR PERCY
(*Recoiling.*) Whatcher mean, nobody's lookin'? (*Indicates audience.*) What about the bozos out there? They could snap me on their mobiles and have me on YouTube, quick as a flash. So even if I fancied yer . . . which I *don't* . . . I wouldn't kiss yer in front of *that* lot.

MRS CRUSOE
(*Resignedly.*) Oh, alright, then. If you're too embarrassed to kiss me in front of the boys and girls . . . we'll go round the back of that palm tree over there and you can kiss me behind.

MUSIC No. 12 (MRS CRUSOE *and* SIR PERCY)

> (*After the song,* SIR PERCY *quickly exits L., with* MRS CRUSOE *in pursuit. As they exit the lights fade to end the scene.*)

Scene Two: A Path Through the Jungle.

A lane scene depicting lush tropical undergrowth, tree trunks and brilliant orchids. Subdued lighting. Enter ROBINSON *and* POLLY *R.*

ROBINSON
(*Wearily.*) No sign of *anyone*, and we've been searching for *hours*.

POLLY
But there must be *someone* here. Remember the *footprint* we found.

ROBINSON
The trouble is, this jungle seems to go on forever. If anyone *is* here, we could easily miss them.

POLLY
Perhaps Billy's had better luck?

ROBINSON
I hope so, because it won't be long before night falls, and we've yet to fmd somewhere to shelter.

POLLY
(*Glances off L., then gives a startled gasp.*) Oh!

ROBINSON
(*Anxiously.*) What is it?

POLLY
(*Still looking L.*) There's someone coming towards us.

> (*As* ROBINSON *turns to look,* DISPRIN, *hurries on L. She is a teenage girl in a brightly coloured sarong, There is a hibiscus flower in her hair, and she has bare feet.*)

DISPRIN
(*Seeing them.*) Oh! (*Turns as if to exit again, then turns back.*) Please. *Please*. Don't tell anyone you've seen me. They'll only want to take me back to the palace and I *won't* go. I just *won't*.

ROBINSON
(*Surprised.*) There's a *palace* on the island?

DISPRIN
(*Equally surprised.*) Well, of course there is. It's the most beautiful palace in the world.

POLLY
Then why are you running away from it?

DISPRIN
Because I don't want to marry that horrible old *man*, of course. (*Sadly.*) Oh, why was I born a Princess?

ROBINSON
(*Startled.*) *Princess?*

(*He and* POLLY *exchange glances.*)

DISPRIN
(*Surprised.*) Princess *Disprin*. Don't you *recognise* me?

ROBINSON
I'm afraid not. We were shipwrecked during last night's storm, and only arrived here this morning. Crusoe's the name. *Robinson* Crusoe. (*Bows, then indicates* POLLY.) And this is *Polly Perkins*, my fiancée.

(POLLY *curtsies.*)

DISPRIN
(*Dismayed.*) Oh, *no*. (*Glances around quickly.*) Then *you* need to hide, as well. You've no *idea* how much danger you're in. Everyone on the island's looking for you. If you're *found*, they'll *have* to take you to the Palace so that dreadful old *monster* can kill you.

ROBINSON
(*Puzzled.*) Your father's a *monster?*

DISPRIN
No, no. My mother, Queen *Paracetamol*, should rule Migrainia. but when *he* arrived here, thousands of years ago, he overthrew her and claimed the throne for himself. Since *then*, everyone who's ever *landed* on the island's been trapped by one of his magic spells. And though he *does* go away for years on end, whenever he comes back, we have to do exactly as he says.

POLLY
(*Awed.*) You mean . . . everyone on the island's *immortal?*

DISPRIN
Yes. But *now* he's looking for a *wife*, and I'm the one he's chosen.

POLLY
How *awful*. (*Puzzled.*) But who *is* he?

DISPRIN
Davy *Jones*, of course.

ROBINSON
(*Frowning.*) You mean . . . as in the old *legend?*

(DAVY *enters L., in a green spotlight. All react.*)

DAVY
(*Triumphantly.*) Who else? The one each sailor fears
Will leave his sweetheart shedding tears,
While *he's* reposing fathoms deep,
In everlasting dreamless sleep. (*Cackles.*)

ROBINSON
(*Unimpressed.*) Is this a *joke*, or something? Davy Jones doesn't *exist*. He's
only a *myth* . . . like Unicorns, fairies, and honest politicians.

DAVY
(*Snarling.*) Yer think so, eh? Well take my word,
Yer information's quite absurd.
I'll prove right *now* it's tommy-rot
And strike yer *dead* upon the spot. (*Raises his arms to cast a spell.*)

(POLLY *and* DISPRIN *cower.*)

ROBINSON
(*Unconcerned.*) Well . . . if you were *really* Davy Jones, I suppose you
could *do* it. (*Shrugs.*) But as you're only a mirage and not really *here* . . .
I can't say I'm worried.

DAVY
(*Puzzled.*) Not *here,* yer say? (*To audience.*) The boy's gone *mad.*
He's lost his wits, this Yorkshire lad, (*Incredulously.*)
And furthermore, he shows no fear.
He truly thinks that I'm not here.

ROBINSON
(*Amused.*) Well, it's *obvious*, you're not, isn't it? And I can *prove* it.

(DAVY *looks at him in astonishment.*)

ROBINSON
(*Off-handedly.*) You're not in *China*, are you?

(DAVY *shakes his head.*)

And you're not in *Spain?*

(DAVY *shakes his head.*)

(*Reasonably.*) So if you're not in China, and you're not in Spain, you must be somewhere *else*, mustn't you?

DAVY
(*Sarcastically.*) I knows you mortals ain't too bright . . . (*Frowns.*)
But just fer *once* . . . I think yer *right*. (*Tries to solve the puzzle.*)

ROBINSON
Then in *that* case . . . if you're somewhere *else*, you can't possibly be *here*, can you?

DAVY
(*Thinking wildly.*) Be quiet, and give me time to *think*.
Me concentration's on the blink
(*Confused.*) Me head's a-whirl. His logic's *right*.
(*Horrified.*) I *must* be somewhere else tonight. (*Clutches at his head.*)
Me brain's gone soft as cherry jam.
Quick, someone tell me where I *am*.

ROBINSON
(*Offhandedly.*) It's no use asking *me*. I'm just a sailor. You could be in Alaska for all *I* know.

DAVY
(*Horrified.*) *Alaska?* Land of snow and frost? (*Moans pitifully.*)
Saints preserve me. Davy's *lost*.
(*Staggering.*) Me bearings' gone. I'm all at sea.
Wherever can old Davy *be?*

(*Totters off L., weakly and the green light goes out.*)

POLLY
(*Relieved.*) Oh, *Robinson*. (*Gives him a quick hug.*) You've driven him off.

DISPRIN
(*Amazed.*) You're the bravest man in the *world*.

ROBINSON
(*Embarrassed.*) Not really. He's just a *bully* in *my* opinion . . . and a
rather *stupid* one, too. And *all* bullies are cowards when you stand up to
them. That's something I was taught at school.

DISPRIN
(*Curiously.*) *School?* What's *that?*

POLLY
(*Puzzled.*) Surely you've been to *school*.

DISPRIN
(*Blankly.*) No.

ROBINSON
It's where they *teach* things. Like Reading and Writing.

POLLY
And History, and Maths.

DISPRIN
(*Doubtfully.*) Oh. I don't think I'd like *that*. (*Dreamily.*) I'd sooner pick
flowers, swim in the sea and count all the stars at night.

POLLY
(*Curious.*) But how did you learn *anything* if you didn't go to school?

DISPRIN
(*Pertly.*) I don't *have* to learn anything. I'm a *princess*.

ROBINSON
But even *princesses* need to know what's *good* for them.

DISPRIN
Not this one.

MUSIC No. 13 (PRINCESS DISPRIN, *or* ROBINSON *and* POLLY, *with* DISPRIN
joining in, if so required.)

        (*After the song, they all exit R., and the lights fade as
        the scene ends.*)

Scene Three: The Palace Gardens.

A full set depicting an exotic garden, with tropical palms, flowers, etc, and a large fountain in the background. Entrances and exits are masked by ruined stonework, or huge flowering plants. Upstage C. is an ornate garden seat, and on this sits QUEEN PARACETAMOL. *She is full of life and swathed in a brilliantly multi-coloured gown of ruffles and beads, topped with a towering hat of tropical fruits, a la the 1940s film star, Carmen Miranda. On top of all this is a small gold crown. Servants in Egyptian-style costume are wafting her gently with huge feather fans on poles, and when the scene begins, she and the Migrainians, in their various national costumes, are watching a group of dancers, in silky, Eastern-based costumes, performing a short exotic dance routine to a throbbing beat.*

MUSIC No. 14 (DANCERS)

As their dance comes to an end, the music segues into another throbbing intro, and she rises and sashays her way down to C.F. As the dancers back away L. and R.

MUSIC No. 15 (QUEEN, *and possibly* CHORUS)

When the song ends, CODINE *enters down R. and she gestures him to approach. He moves to her side as the others form small groups and chatter silently in the background.*

QUEEN
(*Confidentially.*) Any news, *yet*, Lord Chamberlain?

CODINE
(*Confidentially.*) Not a *word*, Your Majesty. Though they're still searching.

QUEEN
(*Anxiously.*) But not *too* hard, I hope?

CODINE
Definitely not, Your Majesty. I told them to do it with their eyes closed.

QUEEN
(*Satisfied.*) Good. (*Firmly.*) I will *not* have my lovely daughter carried off by that malevolent monstrosity, Davy Jones.

CODINE
Well if what that fairy said is *true* . . . he won't have *time* to carry her off.

QUEEN
(*Kindly.*) Oh, Codine. You're so kind and gentle, but maybe it's time you thought about retiring? This *is* the eighteenth century, after all. Everyone *knows* there're no such things as fairies.

CODINE
(*Protesting.*) But Your Majesty . . .

QUEEN
Oh, I'm sure you think you saw one . . . Men have such wonderful imaginations. Take my late husband, for instance. *He* thought he'd found a way of escaping from the island, and fetching help.

CODINE
(*Interested.*) What was it?

QUEEN
(*Lowering her voice.*) He found a magic carpet on one of the shipwrecks, and one Sunday morning, set off for the British Isles.

CODINE
(*Lowering his voice.*) And what *happened*, Your Majesty?

QUEEN
Well . . . he was fine until he found himself ten thousand metres over (*Local village or town.*), then *suddenly* . . . a hole opened up in the middle of the carpet, and he fell straight through it.

(CODINE *reacts, wide-eyed.*)

But luckily he was wearing a *parachute* . . . and quick as a flash he pulled the rip-cord, and a few minutes later . . . *splat.* Made a ten-foot deep hole in the middle of the High Street.

CODINE
(*Stunned.*) You mean . . . his parachute didn't *open?*

QUEEN
(*Shakes her head.*) *Nothing* opens in (*Local village or town again.*) on a Sunday. (*Brightly.*) But I *do* like a good *story* . . . and what you said about the fairy really cheered me up. Just think . . . if there *was* such a person as Robinson Crusoe . . . and he *did* get rid of Davy Jones for us

. . . the spell would break, I'd be a *real* queen again and everyone could go back to where they came from.

CODINE

(*Sighing.*) But would they want to, Your Majesty? Some of them have been here for hundreds of years, and everyone they loved will be long gone.

QUEEN

(*Deflated.*) You're right, of course. (*Unhappily.*) Oh, Codine. I'm all depressed, now. Let's walk round the garden and look at the flowers. Maybe *they'll* make me feel better.

> (*She moves down L, with* CODINE *following closely, and they exit.* MIGRAINIANS *begin to exit up L. and R. As soon as they have gone,* BILLY *cautiously enters down R.*)

BILLY

(*To audience.*) Hiya, kids. (*Audience response, and he looks round in awe.*) So *this* is the Chelsea Flower Show. (*Gives a sigh of relief.*) Ooooh, thank goodness I'm here in one piece. You wouldn't *believe* what's just happened to me. I got chased through the jungle by a big white *crispy* thing, swinging from tree to tree, and showing its teeth, like this. (*Demonstrates.*) It must have been a meringue-outan. And it's a really *funny* place, this island. Everywhere you go, there's great big statues carved out of rock. Our Robinson says they're just the kind of things people travel thousands of miles to see when they're searching for dead civilizations. I don't know why they *bother*. They should just go to (*Local town or village.*) But I can't stand here talking when I'm supposed to be looking for my *mum*. (*Worried.*) Ooooh. I hope she's all right.

> (*Enter* HALE *and* HEARTY *up R. They are both smothered in gold medallions, jewelled necklaces, earrings, bracelets and tiaras, carrying the treasure chest, which is still closed but is now displaying a broken lock. An invisible wire is now attached to the L. side of the chest, and goes off L.*)

BOTH

(*Deliriously singing as they enter.*) We're in the money. We're in the money. (*They do a joyful on-the-spot jig.*)

BILLY

(*Impressed.*) Blimey. Where did you find *that?*

HALE

(*Halting.*) Floating in the water when the ship sank. And it's filled to the brim with gold coins and jewels. (*Chortles.*)

(*They put the chest down and move down to him.*)

BILLY

(*Enviously.*) Oooh, you lucky things. And what are you going to do with it?

HALE

(*Gleefully.*) Well as soon as we get back home, *I'm* going to buy the world's biggest television set, and watch *reality* shows all day long.

BILLY

(*Puzzled.*) What's a *reality* show?

HALE

(*Surprised.*) Have you not *seen* one? (*Enthusiastically.*) Ooooh, you don't know what you're *missing.* They're the kind of shows where you see *real* policemen chasing *real* car thieves and burglars, and breaking down doors to catch illegal immigrants and drug dealers.

BILLY

(*Scornfully.*) You don't need a television set for *that.* Come to live in *our* street, and you can just look out of the window.

HEARTY

(*Happily.*) And *I'm* going to Paris again. (*Sings a snatch of a French-sounding song.*)

HALE

(*Surprised.*) What do you mean, *again?* I didn't know you'd *been* there in the first place.

HEARTY

Oh, yes. I went through the Channel Tunnel and saw the Eyeful Tower, the Boys de balloons *and* the Champs Deleezy. (*Smirks.*)

BILLY

And didn't you go to the Louvre?

HEARTY

(*Regretfully.*) Not once, all week. I think it was the change of water.

HALE

(*Breezily.*) Well, cheerio, mate. *We're* heading back to Hull to sell all this treasure.

BILLY

(*Surprised.*) How can you do *that?* The ship's at the bottom of the sea.

HEARTY

Yes. But we found a brand new lifeboat on the beach, and if we chop it up and build a raft, we can be home in no time.

(*Enter* SIR PERCY *L.*)

SIR PERCY

(*Angrily.*) But not with *my* treasure, yer sniveling, slimy, sea-slugs. I *knewd* you was after it, the minute yer begged me ter take yer on board. (*Brandishes the stick.*) Stand still while I bash you.

(HALE *and* HEARTY *retreat backwards hastily to the chest.*)

HALE

(*Protesting weakly.*) But we didn't *know* it was yours, Sir Percy. (*Quickly lifts the lid and hastily strips off his adornments, throwing them into the chest.*)

HEARTY

We'd no *idea.* (*Following suit.*)

SIR PERCY

(*Roaring.*) How could yer *not* know, yer saponaceous scavengers? It's the biggest chest in the world. (*Advances on them, slashing with his stick.*)

(*Enter* MRS CRUSOE *R., in another fantastic creation.*)

MRS CRUSOE

(*Archly.*) Saucy! Talking about *me* again?

(SIR PERCY *halts and turns to her.*)

BILLY

(*Relieved.*) Mum! I thought you'd been drownded.

MRS CRUSOE

(*Scornfully.*) Course I've not been *drownded.* The minute I hit the water, I was off like an atomic sumberine.

BILLY
(*Surprised.*) Then what took you so long? The others arrived *ages* before *you* did.

MRS CRUSOE
Well . . . I was doing the breast stroke . . . and they were using their arms. (*Remembering.*) Mind you . . . I *nearly* didn't make it. I'd only gone half a mile when somebody threw a pork pie at me. And when I didn't stop, they threw a chicken sandwich, two muffins, a packet of crisps and a bottle of coca cola.

BILLY
(*Amazed.*) And who *was* it?

MRS CRUSOE
(*Airily.*) Just somebody trying to *hamper me.* (*Beams.*) Still . . . I'm here now, so there's nothing to worry about. (*Notices the treasure chest.*) Oooh, I say. (*To* SIR PERCY.) Is that the chest you were looking for? I hope there's something in it for *me?* (*Moves up to it.*)

SIR PERCY
(*Sourly.*) No, there ain't. (*Hurries up to her.*) There's nothing in it at all. (*Slams down the lid.*) 'Specially for you.

HALE
(*Helpfully.*) There's a size sixteen mink coat.

SIR PERCY
(*Grudgingly.*) Well . . . Yer *could* have *that,* I suppose. (*Firmly.*) But not fer *nothing.* If I gives out presents to a *female,* I usually asks fer a *kiss.*

MRS CRUSOE
(*Incredulously.*) You must be joking! A size sixteen mink coat in exchange for one of my kisses? (*Grandly.*) For your inflamation, I'm not that kind of girl. (*Sticks her nose in the air.*)

HEARTY
(*Curious.*) What kind *are* you, then?

MRS CRUSOE
A size *eight.* (*Pushes* SIR PERCY *playfully and sends him flying.*)

(*Enter* ROBINSON *and* POLLY, R. *followed by* DISPRIN.)

ROBINSON
(*Relieved.*) Mother! Thank goodness you're safe.

MRS CRUSOE
(*Delightedly.*) Oh, it's my *eldest*! With Polly Perkins and . . . (*Notices* DISPRIN.) Who's *this?*

DISPRIN
(*Proudly.*) I am Princess *Disprin*. And my mother, Queen Paracetamol is the rightful ruler of Migrania.

(HALE *and* HEARTY *quickly curtsey.*)

MRS CRUSOE
(*Impressed.*) Oh, I say. Fancy me, meeting a *princess.* Mind you . . . I've met famous people *before*. I met *James Bond*, once.

ROBINSON
(*Surprised.*) Really?

MRS CRUSOE
Oh, yes. It was at a Garden Party. I had a little stall with a notice over it, saying "A kiss from the prettiest girl in Yorkshire for only 5p."

BILLY
(*Impressed.*) And he *bought* one?

MRS CRUSOE
No. He walked straight past me.

POLLY
Then how did you know who he was?

MRS CRUSOE
Because I heard him say "If *she's* the prettiest girl in Yorkshire, *I'm* James Bond."

SIR PERCY
(*Snarling.*) Bah! I ain't got no time fer film stars and the like. Ain't never bin to a cinema in me *life*.

DISPRIN
Me neither. (*Wryly.*) I don't even know what a cinema *is.*

BILLY
It's where you go for entertainment if you haven't got Sky television.

HALE
Oooh, I *love* the cinema, I do. I used to go every week when I was little.
It was ever so cheap, then.

HEARTY
Yes. If you wore *long* pants, it was only ten pence admission . . . and if
you wore *short* pants, you could go in for *five.*

MRS CRUSOE
I wish *I'd* known that. I could have gone in for *nothing.*

ROBINSON
Well never mind the *cinema.* Princess Disprin's just given us some
terrible news.

BILLY
(*Dismayed.*) Don't say the (*Local newspaper*)'s Drama Critic's in tonight.

ROBINSON
No, no. It's *far* worse than *that.*

MRS CRUSOE
(*Horrified.*) He / She's not coming at *all?*

ROBINSON
(*Heavily.*) *Apparently* there's a *spell* on the island, and once you're *here,*
you're unable to leave again.

POLLY
And not only *that* . . . All its *water* comes from the Fountain of Youth . . .
and if you *drink* it, you'll never get any older.

MRS CRUSOE
(*Delightedly.*) Ooooh. Does that mean I'll always be twenty-seven?

SIR PERCY
(*Scornfully.*) Bah! Ain't no such thing as a Fountain of *Youth.* If it *did*
exist . . . the water'd be worth more than all the treasure in this chest.

> (MRS CRUSOE *attempts to open the lid, but* SIR PERCY
> *slaps at her hand with his stick. She hastily lets go.*)

HEARTY
Not to me, it wouldn't. I'd sooner be *rich* than young. They only offer
you *rotten* jobs when you're young.

ROBINSON
(*Puzzled.*) How do you work *that* out?

HEARTY
I went to be a *postman* once, but when they asked me if I knew how far it was from London to Glasgow, I told them to forget it and walked out.

POLLY
Didn't you know the *answer?*

HEARTY
'Course I did. But who wants a round *that* big?

ROBINSON
(*Firmly.*) There is one *other* thing. Though Queen Paracetamol *should* rule the Island, everyone *on* it's the prisoner of Davy Jones and unless someone gets the better of him and breaks his spell, we'll never see England again.

(*Everyone reacts.*)

SIR PERCY
(*Aghast.*) Davy *Jones,* yer say? (*Stunned.*) Then we're *done* for. Ain't *nobody* gets the better of *him.*

(*Enter* QUEEN *and* CODINE *R.*)

QUEEN
(*Surprised.*) Disprin! You're back again. But who are these *people?*

DISPRIN
(*Turning to her, delightedly.*) Oh, mother. They're the people from last night's shipwreck.

(*All bow or curtsey.*)

And this (*Indicates* ROBINSON.) is the man who rescued me from Davy Jones. (*Happily.*) Mr Robinson *Crusoe.*

QUEEN
(*Taken aback.*) Crusoe? (*To* CODINE, *delightedly.*) Oh, *Codine.* He's *here.* He's really here. Spread the news *quickly.* We're going to be *saved.* (*Laughs delightedly.*)

(CODINE *totters off R. hastily as others look puzzled.*)

QUEEN
(*To* DISPRIN.) And the minute the spell's broken, we'll have the biggest party the world's ever seen. (*To* ROBINSON, *excitedly.*) How are you going to *do* it?

ROBINSON
(*Confused.*) Do *what*, Your Majesty?

QUEEN
Get rid of Davy Jones, of course.

ROBINSON
(*Baffled.*) I've no idea.

QUEEN
(*Protesting.*) But you *must* have. The fairy said you'd finish him off and we'd all be free again.

(*Everyone looks baffled.*)

ROBINSON
It's the first *I've* heard about it. I don't even *believe* in fairies.

MRS CRUSOE
(*Hastily.*) Oooh, you mustn't say things like *that,* Robinson. (*Comes forward.*) Of course there's such things as fairies. Your Uncle Cyril met one last year.

BILLY
(*Accusingly.*) You never told *us* that.

MRS CRUSOE
How could I? Robinson was stuck on his desert island, and *you* were out every night playing your trumpet in Hull orchestra.

POLLY
(*To* BILLY, *amazed.*) *You* played trumpet in the *orchestra?*

BILLY
(*Modestly.*) Only for a bit. But I had to give it up 'cos every time we finished a concert, I'd have great big lumps on the back of my head.

QUEEN
Were you *allergic* to something?

BILLY
No. I sat in front of the trombone players. (*To* MRS CRUSOE.) But what's all this about Uncle Cyril meeting a fairy?

MRS CRUSOE
Well . . . he was sitting up in bed one night, changing the oil in his motor bike, when suddenly, there was a great big flash, and there she was. A real live fairy. "Mr Crusoe," she said. "You're such a nice, kind man, I've decided to give you three wishes. Whatever you want shall be yours at once."

ROBINSON
(*Curious.*) And what did he wish for?

MRS CRUSOE
Well the *first* thing was to be young and handsome again. So she waved her wand, and there he was . . . fifty years younger, and looking exactly like Daniel Radcliffe (*Or other well known actor*).

(*All react.*)

And then he wished to have more money than anyone else in the world, and a second later, he was surrounded by gold bars, sack-fulls of cash and jewels, and bundles and bundles of expenses claim sheets from the Houses of Parliament.

(*All react again.*)

And *finally* . . . he wished to be irresistible to women.

SIR PERCY
(*Sneering.*) An yer not tellin' us *that* happened?

MRS CRUSOE
I am. One wave of her wand . . . and he turned into a block of chocolate.

ROBINSON
Well fairy or no fairy, I don't see what *I* can do to help.

(*The lights dim and* Davy *enters down L. in his usual green light. All react.*)

DAVY
How right you are. Against *my* powers *no* mortal can prevail.
Oppose me, and I hereby swears they'll never *live* to tell the tale.

So on yer knees, I wants ter see due homage to me rendered
(*To audience.*) An' as fer *you* lot . . . sling yer hooks.
Yer pantomime's just ended. (*Cackles nastily.*)

(*Enter* FAIRY *D.R., in a white light. All react.*)

FAIRY
(*To* DAVY.) Again you *leap* before you *look*. It's really rather tragic.
For nothing's sadder than the foe who'd mock the Coral Fairy's magic.
Take my word. Young Robinson will turn your dreams to ashes.
And all your "Castles in the air" knock down with mighty crashes.

DAVY
(*Sneering.*) You lie. You lie. I've looked it up upon the Internet.
And *Google*, which is *never* wrong, declares I'm *far* from finished, yet.
Protected by an ancient charm, I'm safe from ev'ry kind of harm.
(*Chuckles gleefully.*)

FAIRY
Not *quite*. Your goose can soon be cooked, by something *Google* overlooked.
All magic spells become forsworn, when challenged by a *Unicorn*.

DAVY
(*Amused.*) But unicorns . . . as well you know . . . are easy to resist.
And why? *Because,* you foolish fay, those creatures never *did* exist.
So wave yer wand and cast yer spells, I ain't the least concerned.
Leave Master Crusoe up ter *me* . . . and watch him get his fingers burned.
(*Cackles.*)

FAIRY
If *that's* the case, it would appear you *still* think you've the upper hand.
And Neptune's wishes will ignore by using tactics underhand.
So be it, then. The die is cast. Of me, it seems, you've seen the last.

(*Exits R. and the white light goes out.*)

ROBINSON
(*Calling anxiously.*) But what about *us?*

DAVY
(*Smirks.*) I'll deal with *you* before the dawn. But first, I claim my bride . . .
(*Leers at* DISPRIN.) Come closer, lovely lady, and stand here by my side.

(DISPRIN *recoils in horror.*)

MRS CRUSOE
(*Indignantly.*) You must be jolting. I'm not marrying *you*. I've seen better looking frogspawn.

>   (DAVY *points at* DISPRIN, *and a green spotlight captures her. She falls into a trance and he slowly rotates his hand. She moves towards him as though sleepwalking. All react.*)

QUEEN
(*Alarmed.*) Somebody *save* her.

>   (DAVY *gestures again, and all freeze, unable to move.*)

DAVY
(*Triumphantly.*) Too late. The Princess now is mine.
We'll wed without delay. (*Takes her arm.*)
In Davy's Locker, neath the waves,
We'll celebrate our *Bridal Day.*

>   (*Cackles with glee and exits, taking the un-protesting* DISPRIN *with him. The green lights go out, other lighting returns to its original settings, and the* COMPANY *unfreeze.*)

POLLY
He's *gone.*

SIR PERCY
(*Relieved.*) But at least he's left me *treasure* behind. (*Indicates the chest.*)

>   (*The treasure chest is suddenly bathed in a green light, and shoots off L. into the wings. The green light goes out.*)

(*Horrified.*) Aghhhhhhhhhhh. (*Staggers with shock.*)

>   (MIGRAINIANS *re-enter L. and R. and fill the background as the dialogue continues.* CODINE *enters down R.*)

BILLY
(*Dismayed.*) *That's* torn it. We can't leave the island. Fairy Liquid's gone back to where she came from. Davy Crockett's kidnapped Princess Whatsit . . .

(MIGRAINIANS *react with shocked silent muttering.*)

. . . and we haven't a penny left between us. Doesn't anything *nice* happen here?

MRS CRUSOE
(*Happily.*) Well if we can find this Fountain of Youth, I'll never have to put twenty-eight candles on my birthday cake.

QUEEN
(*Upset.*) What am I going to *do?* (*To* ROBINSON.) I was told you'd arrived here to *save* Migrainia, yet what have you done so far? Nothing at all. And now my only daughter's been carried off by that dreadful *monster.* (*Wails.*)

                    (MIGRAINIANS *murmur as* HALE *and* HEARTY *grimace
                    theatrically.*)

ROBINSON
(*Bravely.*) Don't worry, Your Majesty. I've no idea *how* I'm going to do it but if that really *was* a fairy we saw a few minutes ago, she must have known what she was talking about. So I'm willing to take my chances.

                    (QUEEN *and* MIGRAINIANS *brighten.* MRS CRUSOE, BILLY
                    and POLLY *look concerned.*)

If *you'll* take care of my friends, *I'll* go after *him* this very minute.

POLLY
(*Protesting.*) But what can you *do?* If nothing but a *unicorn* can harm him, and unicorns don't *exist*, you haven't a hope.

ROBINSON
There's *always* hope, Polly. And with a bit of luck, both the Princess and I will be back before morning.

BILLY
(*Anxiously.*) You don't want *me* to come, do you? 'Cos I've got a hole in me sock, and me left trunnion's got a perforated blandishment.

ROBINSON
No, no. You stay here and look after Mum and Polly. By the look of things, this is *my* moment, and win or lose, I'm going to make the very most of it.

MUSIC No. 16 (ROBINSON – *with* COMPANY?)

> (*At the end of the song, there is a rapid fade to end the scene.*)

Scene Four: A Cave on the Seashore.

A lane scene. Backdrop represents the interior of a seashore cave. Gloomy lighting. Enter DAVY L. in a green light, followed by the still enchanted PRINCESS DISPRIN. He moves C. She remains a short distance away from him, unseeing.

DAVY
(*Sneering.*) Still here, I see? Well, suit yourselves.
I *told* you all to go.
You'll not leave here with happy smiles . . .
It ain't that kind of show.
(*Smirking.*) The only one who's havin' fun
Is *me.* And I'm delighted.
I'm getting wed, this very night . . .
And *you* lot aren't invited. (*Cackles and exits R., followed by* PRINCESS.)

> (*The green light goes out. Enter* ROBINSON, *L., warily.*)

ROBINSON
Thank goodness Friday taught me how to track. I don't know where they're *going*, but they definitely came into this *cave.* (*Glancing around.*) And it must lead under the *sea.* There's *salt-water* dripping from the roof. (*Uneasily.*) Not only that . . . it's getting colder and darker. If they go much further, I could lose them altogether. Why didn't I bring a *torch?* (*Sighing.*) Though that's the *least* of my worries. Even if I do catch up with them, what am I going to do? All I have are my *fists* . . . and if only a *unicorn* can harm him, I'm sure they won't have him trembling with fear. (*Shrugs.*) But it's no use standing here and *worrying.* I'll just follow them as fast as I can. (*Exits R.*)

> (*Enter* BILLY *L., cautiously, followed by* HALE *and* HEARTY.)

BILLY
Hiya, kids. (*Audience reaction.*) Ooooh, Isn't it dark in here?

HALE
(*Grimacing.*) And look at the puddles on the floor. Fall into one of *them*, and we'll all be *sneezing* tomorrow.

BILLY
(*Scornfully.*) Give over. You don't catch colds from being wet.

HEARTY
Don't you?

BILLY
'Course not. *Fish* live in water, don't they? And how many have *you* seen carrying a box of Kleenex? (*Firmly.*) It's *coughs* and *sneezes* that spread diseases. *Everybody* knows that.

HALE
The little girl down *there* doesn't. (*Indicates a spot halfway down the auditorium.*) She sat next to me on the bus, last week, and coughed and sneezed and sniffled all the way to (*Local place*).

HEARTY
Didn't you *say* something?

HALE
(*Indignantly.*) Of course I did. I asked her if she'd got a *handkerchief.*

BILLY
And what did she say?

HALE
"Yes. But I'm not lending it to a dirty old tramp like *you.*"

BILLY
Well never mind about *colds.* We've got to hurry if we're going to catch up with our Robinson. We can't let him fight Davy Jones on his own.

HALE
(*Uneasily.*) But what if it's dangerous?

BILLY
(*Scornfully.*) Doesn't bother *me.* I've got a black belt in Origami.

HEARTY
(*Smugly.*) And when I was in *Africa*, I hunted man-eating lions with a little *club.*

BILLY
(*Impressed.*) I bet *that* was risky.

HEARTY
(*Modestly.*) Not really. There were six of us in the club, and we *all* had *guns.*

MRS CRUSOE
(*Off L.*) Yoo-hoo?

> (MRS CRUSOE *enters L. in another outrageous outfit, and carries a plastic sandwich box. She is followed by a scowling* SIR PERCY.)

(*To* BILLY, *relieved.*) Thank goodness I've found you in time. I've brought some sandwiches for your lunch. (*Holds out the box.*)

BILLY
(*Surprised.*) But you *gave* us a box of sandwiches before we set off.

MRS CRUSOE
I know. But the tins had lost their labels in the shipwreck and with it still being dark, I wasn't sure what I'd opened. You've not eaten 'em, already, have you?

BILLY
'Course we have. And they were *lovely.*

> (HALE *and* HEARTY *agree.*)

MRS CRUSOE
In that case, I don't suppose it matters. But you'll have to polish your shoes with *fish-paste*, tomorrow morning. (*Glancing round.*) Oooh, I say . . . I don't like the look of *this* place. It's like the inside of a black pudding. You could trip up and hurt yourself.

BILLY
Don't worry, Mum. We'll be safe as houses.

MRS CRUSOE
(*Tartly.*) Yes. And if you fall over and break your legs, don't come running to *me*. If Health and Safety knew we'd a scene like *this* in the show, they'd fill the place with floodlights, and make us wear *hard* hats. (*Worried.*) P'raps we should take out *insurance?*

HALE
(*Nodding.*) You're *right*, Mrs Crusoe. We should *all* get insured, shouldn't we? Only last *week*, an insurance seller came knocking on

our door and told us to buy some. "What for?" I said. "Well," he said "Only six months ago, I sold an insurance policy to a customer, and the following *day* he tripped over his cat, fell down the stairs, broke his neck and *died. Our company* paid out five hundred pounds, and you could be just as *lucky.*"

SIR PERCY
(*Gloomily.*) Ain't no insurance gonna get my *treasure chest* back.

MRS CRUSOE
(*Dismissively.*) You don't need insurance for *that*, love. Just wait 'til my Robinson's polished off Davy Jones, and you'll be able to keep me in comfort for the rest of my life. (*Beams at him.*)

SIR PERCY
(*Startled.*) Keep *you* in comfort?

MRS CRUSOE
Well you *do* want to *marry* me, don't you?

SIR PERCY
(*Outraged.*) *I* want to *marry* you?

MRS CRUSOE
I *knew* you did, so I accept. (*Puckers her lips at him and he recoils hastily.*)

BILLY
(*Impatiently.*) There'll be nobody marrying *anybody* if we don't catch up with our Robinson. (*Indicates R.*) He'll be miles in front, now.

HEARTY
(*Unhappily.*) Yes. But I don't fancy going any further into *this* cave. We don't know what's *in* there. It could be a *bear.* And what would we do if it *chased* us?

HALE
I know what *I'd* do if a bear chased us. I'd run back to the Palace.

MRS CRUSOE
(*Surprised.*) What? With a bear behind?

SIR PERCY
(*Snarling.*) Aghhhh. Yer'll not find a bear in a sea-cave. Most yer'll get in *this* place is lobsters an' spider-crabs.

BILLY
(*Nervously.*) Ooooh. I don't like the sound of *them*.

HEARTY
Me neither. I was paddling at the seaside once, and a lobster pinched my *toe*.

HALE
Which one?

HEARTY
How do *I* know? All lobsters look the same to me.

SIR PERCY
Well yer don't have to fret about *sea-life* nipping yer tootsies. Take it from Sir Percy . . . they can't stand 'umans *singing*. I read about it on Wikipedia. Gets 'em shivverin' in their shells, it does. So all yer 'ave ter do is sing at the top of yer voices, and they won't come near yer.

MRS CRUSOE
(*Surprised.*) Oh, I say . . . I never knew *that*. Well that's all right, then. We've nothing to worry about.

BILLY
(*Unsure.*) I don't know. It's dark down here, and what if something comes scuttling up *behind* us? We wouldn't see it coming.

HALE
(*Nervously.*) He's right.

MRS CRUSOE
(*Cheerfully.*) Well we can soon change *that*. We'll ask all the boys and girls in the audience to *warn* us. (*To audience.*) You'll do that, won't you?

(*Audience response.*)

HEARTY
(*Uneasily.*) They don't sound all that sure.

SIR PERCY
'Course they *is*. (*To audience, menacingly.*) An' if yer *doesn't* warn us . . . I'll fix it that all yer school dinners'll be nothin' but platefuls of soggy *sprouts* and *snail porridge*.

(*All grimace with revulsion.*)

BILLY
Well what are we going to sing, then?

HALE
How about, "Get out the beans and sausages . . . there's a fork in the road ahead"?

MRS CRUSOE
(*Scornfully.*) No, *no.* We don't want old fashioned songs like *that.* We need something *modern.*

HEARTY
What about something by Elton John?

BILLY
(*Scornfully.*) How can we sing something by Elton *John?* It's only the eighteenth century. He hasn't been *born* yet.

SIR PERCY
Tell you what, comrades . . . We'll sing something we *all* know. Ten Green Bottles. *That*'ll keep the nasties away.

(*All agree.*)

MRS CRUSOE
And we'll have a little practice before we set off. Just to make sure we all know the words. (*To audience.*) And don't forget . . . if you see anything creeping up behind us . . . shout at the top of your voices.

BILLY
Off we go then. One, two, three.

(*They commence singing. After a moment, a huge* SEA MONSTER *lurches in L. bathed in a green light. It moves behind them, dripping with seaweed and displaying a large fishing net on a pole. As the audience reacts, it moves R. and exits. The green light goes out and the group stop singing in some confusion.*)

MRS CRUSOE
(*To audience.*) No, no. You haven't understood me. You don't scream when we're *singing.* (*Chuckles.*) We're not the Rolling *Stones.* (*Or other well known group.*) You only scream when you see something *nasty.*

BILLY
(*Uneasily.*) I don't know about *seeing* something nasty . . . (*Indicates into the auditorium.*) I think the woman down here's *done* something nasty. I hope she's got a spare pair in her *handbag.*

HALE
We'll have another go, shall we?

HEARTY
They'll know how to do it right, this time.

BILLY
(*Counting.*) One, two, three.

> (*They begin singing again. The* CREATURE *enters R., as before, crosses behind them, and exits L. as the audience react. The group stop singing again.*)

SIR PERCY
(*Glowering.*) What are they on about *now?* I were havin' fun, smashin' them bottles.

MRS CRUSOE
Maybe they're *foreigners?* I'll undress 'em in their own language. (*To audience, with great emphasis.*) Fer-may de booshery when us is vochi-carler-ating. Shutta di gobbo 'til Tony Blair (*Or other disliked personage.*) arreev. (*To others.*) There. I think *that* should do it. I'm very good with foreign languages. I can even understood the ones who come from (*Local town, village or area*).

HALE
Off we go again, then. (*Counts.*) One, two, three.

> (*They begin singing again.* CREATURE *enters L., as before and hovers behind them. As audience react, the singers grind to a halt.*)

BILLY
(*Put out.*) What is it now? What are you shouting for? (*Audience reaction.*) You've seen a *swing?* (*To others.*) They've seen a swing.

> (*Others look amused.*)

(*Tiredly.*) Oh, come on, kids. Stop messing us about. You don't get swings in caves. And besides . . . What's that? (*Pretends to listen.*)

You didn't say a *swing?* You said a *thing?* (*Looks uneasy, then turns to others.*) They didn't say a *swing.* They said a *thing.*

> (*Others look at each other uncertainly.*)

HALE
What . . . er . . . what *sort* of thing?

> (*Audience response.*)

BILLY
(*After "listening" for a moment, unhappily.*) A great big *slimy* thing.

> (*The singers huddle together in fear.*)

(*To audience.*) And where did it *go?* (*Audience response.*) Behind us??? (*To singers, without turning.*) It's behind us.

> (*All freeze in position, petrified looks on their faces.*)

HEARTY
(*Tearfully.*) What are we going to *do?*

SIR PERCY
Ain't nothing to be a-feared of. It's five against one. We'll count up to three, then all turn and grab it. Right?

ALL
(*Counting.*) One, two, *three.*

> (*As they reach two, the* CREATURE *bobs down. Others turn on three, to see nothing.*)

MRS CRUSOE
(*Turning again, in disgust.*) There's nothing there at all.

HALE
(*Annoyed.*) They've just been trying to scare us.

SIR PERCY
(*Scowling.*) We ain't listnin' to *them* again.

> (CREATURE *stands again, behind them.*)

BILLY

(*To someone in the audience.*) I'm going to tell your mum on *you.* You frightened us all to death.

HEARTY

(*Glowering at audience.*) Rotten things. If I hadn't *already* had an accident, I'd have *had* one.

MRS CRUSOE

(*Firmly.*) Well we'll treat 'em with ignoramus, from now on. Let's carry on with the song.

> (*They begin singing again. The* CREATURE *taps* SIR PERCY *on the shoulder. He looks round, sees the* CREATURE, *screams and rapidly exits L. followed by the* CREATURE, *trying to catch him in the net. The others having not seen this, grind to a halt and look round.*)

BILLY

What was that yell? And where's Sir Percy gone?

MRS CRUSOE

(*Biting her lip.*) Oooh. I bet its those tablets I gave him ten minutes ago.

BILLY

(*Puzzled.*) What tablets?

MRS CRUSOE

You *know.* The ones the doctor gave your dad when he was dying of constipation.

HALE

You can't die of constipation, Mrs Crusoe.

MRS CRUSOE

Well *my* husband did. (*Remembering.*) . . . And oooh, they were ever so *powerful,* those tablets.

HEARTY

But they didn't *work*, did they?

MRS CRUSOE

Yes, they did. He went five times before he passed away . . . and eight time after.

HALE & HEARTY
(*Together.*) Let's sing.

> (*They begin to sing again. The* CREATURE *re-enters L.,
> moves behind them, and taps* HALE *and* HEARTY *on the
> shoulders. They turn, see it, scream and rush off R.,
> followed by the creature waving its net.* BILLY *and* MRS
> CRUSOE, *who have not seen this, stop singing.*)

MRS CRUSOE
(*Looking around, puzzled.*) Oh, I say . . . Where've *they* gone?

BILLY
(*Disgustedly.*) I don't know. But they've left us here all on our own. The
rotten cowards.

MRS CRUSOE
Ooooh, if there's one thing I can't stand it's a coward. The next time I
get married, my new husband will have to be a *hero.*

BILLY
Don't say *that*, mum. You're not *that* bad.

MRS CRUSOE
(*After a reaction.*) Sing.

> (*They begin singing again. The* CREATURE *enters R. and
> moves behind them. It taps* BILLY *on the shoulder. He
> looks round, sees it, then turns back continues singing.
> After a moment, it registers and he turns to see it again.
> He screams and dashes off L. followed by the* CREATURE.
> MRS CRUSOE *stops singing.*)

(*Glancing round, nervously.*) Billy? Billy? (*To audience.*) Ooooh, I
say. Now *he's* gone, as well. (*Remembering.*) Mind you . . . he's always
been the nervous kind. The last time we had a storm in Hull . . . he hid
himself down in the cellar because the *lightning* scared him. "It's no use
hiding down there," I told him." If lightning's going to hit you, it'll hit
you *wherever* you go." "I know that," he said. "But if lightning's going to
hit *me*, it'll have to *look* for me." (*Sighs.*) Oh, well. If there's nobody left,
I'll have to sing on my own. It's a good job I had singing lessons from
Madame Melba. But talk about *jealous.* I asked her advice, once. "I can
cope with all the top notes," I said, "but can you tell me what to do with
my hands while I'm singing?" "Well," she said, " You could try clamping
'em over your mouth."

(She begins singing again. The CREATURE *enters L., stands slightly behind her and taps her on the shoulder. She turns to it The* CREATURE *screams, drops the net and exits hastily L. in terror. For a moment she stands there looking after it, then picks up the net.)*

MRS CRUSOE
(Scornfully.) Music critics!

(There is a blackout, and she exits R. as the scene ends.)

Scene Five: Davy Jones' Locker.

A full set. A vast underwater palace, with white coral pillars, the backdrop depicting a sunken wreck A large shell throne is C.B., perhaps on a small plinth with rocky steps leading up to it. Open treasure chests dot the setting, the contents spilling over the sides. Other golden objects such as over-sized plate-ware and candleabra can also be seen. Most of these can be painted onto the scenery, but a few practical ones should be used. Entrances L. and R. are masked by ruined masonry. Lighting should suggest the ocean depths.

If resources allow, this scene can be enhanced by commencing it with a UV display of undersea life, or treasure chests, open and closed, wooden casks, and other suchlike wreckage. A mixture of both could be amusing, with various marine life chasing, holding, fighting over or wearing the salvage.

MUSIC No. 17 (*UV Compilation*)

Otherwise, it begins with a dance of Seahorses, or Water Sprites in floaty garments in vivid shades.

MUSIC No. 17a (*Dance of the Seahorses or Water Sprites.*)

At the conclusion of whichever, all exit in a flurry as DAVY *enters up L., in his usual green spotlights, pulling the* PRINCESS *behind him.*

DAVY
(Expansively.) Behold my realm beneath the waves
Where lies the wealth each mortal craves.
And where, as Davy's loving bride,
For evermore, yer'll now abide.

DISPRIN
(*Struggling.*) Let go of me. Let go. I'll *never* marry *you*, you revolting
creature.

DAVY
(*Amused.*) Oh, yes, yer will. Yer has no choice.
So stop yer strugglin' and rejoice.
What more could any mortal wish
Than to be *here*, among the fish?

DISPRIN
Never. (*Struggles again.*)

DAVY
(*Firmly.*) But just fer *now*, we've things ter do.
We must invite a *guest* or two.
Make sure the gift list's quite extensive.
And the stuff we want's *expensive* . . .
Call some glossy magazine,
And fer a sum that's quite obscene,
Sell *them* our nuptial *photo-rights*
To pay for all our day's delights.
In short . . . if bills for our wedding are many . . .
It'll hardly cost crafty old Davy a penny.

> (*Cackles and exits down L. pulling the still struggling*
> PRINCESS, *behind him. After a moment,* ROBINSON
> *cautiously enters up R.*)

ROBINSON
(*Warily.*) Where on earth am I? (*Glances round, puzzled.*) It looks as
though I'm *underwater* . . . but I can still *breathe*, so that doesn't make
sense. (*Moves down C.*) But *wherever* this is, there's no sign of Davy
Jones, *or* Princess Disprin. (*Sighs.*) If only *Friday* was here. He'd be *full*
of bright ideas.

> (*Enter* FAIRY *down R., in her white follow spot.*)

FAIRY
Beneath the waves, though close to shore,
You stand upon the ocean floor,
Yet 'til the Old Man of The Sea,
To you and Neptune, bends his knee,
You'll find you have no need for air.
You're quite safe, in my fairy care.

ROBINSON
(*Protesting.*) And how long will it be until *that* happens? Now he's found out he can't be beaten, he's not the least bit worried about me, *or* King Neptune. *You're* the one with magic spells. Why can't *you* do something?

FAIRY
I *could*. 'Twould be a *simple* task
To do *exactly* what you ask
(*Sternly.*) But as he mocks our King for *sport,*
A lesson sharp, he must be taught.
So . . . as *your* name is well respected,
For that task, you've been selected.
(On his home-ground, face-to-face),
To put him *firmly* in his place.
While Ocean-dwellers loudly chortle,
At his downfall . . . by a *mortal.*

ROBINSON
But how am I to *do* it? And what about Princess Disprin?

FAIRY
Don't worry. In your time of need,
You'll find it *easy* to succeed.
And after that, I hereby state,
His powers will all evaporate.

(*She turns and exits R., the white spotlight vanishing.*)

ROBINSON
(*Calling urgently.*) Wait. You still haven't told me . . . (*Glances off L.*) Oh-ho. Someone's coming. I'd better hide. (*Hurries off up R.*)

(*Enter* SIR PERCY, *down L., followed by* HALE *and* HEARTY.)

SIR PERCY
(*Moving C., amazed.*) Where've we got to, now? (*Delightedly.*) Look at all this *treasure.*

HALE
(*Excitedly.*) We must be in Davy Jones' *Locker!*

SIR PERCY
(*Scowling.*) Quick. Grab hold o' one o' them chests, each, and we'll be out of here afore he finds us.

HEARTY
But what about the *Princess?*

SIR PERCY
(*Snarling.*) Forget about *her*! It's the treasure *I'm* after. (*Chortles.*) With all this changed into *cash*, I'll be the *world's* richest man.

HALE
(*Protesting.*) Hang on a minute. Hang on. What about *us?*

SIR PERCY
(*Scornfully.*) *You* two? What do you want money for? Yer too daft to know what ter do with it.

HEARTY
(*Protesting.*) No we're *not*. The minute we get a few pounds together, we're going to buy some *dogs.*

HALE
Yes. We saw an advert in the (*Local paper.*) last week, saying "Dogs for sale. Going cheap." An' as most dogs only *bark*, ones that *"cheep"* must be worth a *fortune.*

SIR PERCY
(*Disgusted.*) Bah. You ain't got the brains yer was born with. Grab them chests, and let's be off.

HEARTY
(*Annoyed.*) Do it yourself. If we're not getting *paid*, we're not carrying *anything.*

SIR PERCY
(*Scowling.*) Please yerselves. I'll keep the lot, then. I'll take *one* on me own, and return fer all the others.

> (*He drags one of the treasure chests off L. As he does so,* BILLY *enters down R.*)

BILLY
(*Moving C.F.*) Hiya kids. (*Audience response.*) Here. You'll never guess who *I've* just seen. Prince Charles. Yes. He was visiting a home for old mermaids, just down the road. Mind you . . . he couldn't believe it when none of them seemed to recognise him. "Do you know who I am?" he asked one old dear. "Don't worry," she said, patting his hand. "The Matron'll tell you." (*Sees the others.*) What are you two doing here?

HALE
We're on strike. We've just found all this treasure, and that rotten old Sir Percy's keeping it all to himself.

HEARTY
Yes. He says we're too daft to know what it's for.

BILLY
Well, you'll just have to prove him *wrong,* won't you?

HALE
How do we do that?

BILLY
Ask him a little *question,* and if he doesn't know the answer, tell him he has to give you some of it.

HEARTY
But what shall we ask him? He knows everything.

BILLY
Try this. My mother had a *baby.* It wasn't my *brother,* and it wasn't my *sister* . . . so who was it?

(*They both look puzzled.*)

HALE / HEARTY
(*Together, shaking their heads.*) No idea.

BILLY
It was *me.*

HALE
(*Admiringly.*) Oooooh. He'll never get that. He'll never get that.

HEARTY
We'll end up with a fortune.

(SIR PERCY *re-enters L. panting, and moves to another chest.* HALE *and* HEARTY *hurry over to him.*)

HALE
Just a minute. Just a minute. If we ask you a question, and you don't know the answer . . . can we have some of the treasure?

SIR PERCY
(*Amused.*) Don't be ridiculous. How could yer know more than *me?* I've won Mastermind, six times in a row. Go on then . . . ask yer question.

HALE
All right, then. My mother had a baby. It wasn't my brother and it wasn't my sister . . . so who was it?

> (*They watch him eagerly as he struggles to find the answer.*)

SIR PERCY
(*Finally admitting defeat.*) All right. I ain't got a clue. Who was it?

HEARTY
(*Triumphantly.*) Billy Crusoe! (*Smirks.*)

> (*Enter* MRS CRUSOE *R. in yet another creation.*)

MRS CRUSOE
(*Flustered.*) Oh, I *say* . . . I'm all of a tizwas.

BILLY
(*Concerned.*) Why? What's happened?

MRS CRUSOE
I've just had a *text message* from a woman in Hull. She had triplets this morning, and the doctor's told her it only happens *once* in a hundred thousand times. (*Fans herself with her hand.*)

BILLY
(*Puzzled.*) So?

MRS CRUSOE
Well . . . It's made me start *wondering.* How did she find time to do her *housework?*

> (*Enter* ROBINSON *R.*)

ROBINSON
(*Astounded.*) Mother! Everybody! What are you doing *here?*

BILLY
We came to help rescue the Princess from Davy Jones.

ROBINSON
(*Groaning.*) Oh, no. You *meant* well, I'm sure, but you're *all* in danger, now. If I don't find a way to get the better of him, *none* of us will ever see England again.

HALE
(*Shrugging.*) Doesn't bother *me*. I'm fed up of England. When we get away from this place, I'm going to live in America and change my name so nobody can find me.

BILLY
Ooooh, I wouldn't do *that*. Not change your *name*.

HALE
Why not?

BILLY
Well . . . there was a feller called *Kissinger* once . . . and he didn't like it, so he changed it to *Smith*. But he couldn't get used to it, so after a week or two, he changed it to *Brown*. Six weeks later he changed it to *Watson,* and a few weeks after *that*, he changed it to *Johnson*.

SIR PERCY
(*Scowling.*) Is there any *point* to all this?

BILLY
Of course there is. He changed his name five more times, and before long, all his friends were wondering who's Kissinger now.

HEARTY
Well you won't get *me* living in foreign places. Not 'til I've found my dad again.

MRS CRUSOE
Found your dad?

HEARTY
Oh, yes. He went to buy a newspaper, twenty years ago, and never came back, I've been searching for him ever since.

MRS CRUSOE
Oh, I say . . . And what's he like?

HEARTY
Watching *television*. Drinking *beer*. Chasing *women*.

ROBINSON
(*Exasperated.*) Oh, *please.* Stop talking and go back to the *Palace.* I can
hear someone approaching.

(*Enter* POLLY, *down R., followed by* QUEEN *and* CODINE.)

(*Surprised.*) Polly!

POLLY
And Queen Paracetamol.

QUEEN
And my Chamberlain, Codine.

ROBINSON
(*In disbelief.*) I don't *believe* it. I thought you were safe in the *palace.*

POLLY
(*Protesting.*) We could hardly just *stay* there, when *you* were risking
your life trying to save the Princess.

QUEEN
And as she's *my* daughter, I've ordered everyone in Migrania to follow
us down here to cheer you on.

ROBINSON
(*Tiredly.*) Which is exactly what I *didn't* want. I was hoping to take him
by surprise . . . but there's not a chance of that now. And I don't even
have a sword or cutlass to *protect* you.

CODINE
You can have my staff of office. (*Holds it out to* ROBINSON.) I made it
from something I found on the beach. It's rather old, but it's got a sharp
point.

ROBINSON
(*Reluctantly.*) It's very kind of you, Lord Chamberlain . . . but I hardly
think *that*'ll frighten him.

(DAVY *enters down L. in his green light.*)

DAVY
(*Smirking.*) Yer right. It *won't.*

(*All see him and react.*)

DAVY
Me trap's been sprung.
And them who'd *sting*, will now be *stung*.
(*Triumphantly.*) I *knewed* yer'd foller where I led,
And in me footsteps quickly tread.
Now say yer prayers and close yer eyes . . .
Today's the day the whole lot *dies*. (*Lifts his arms to cast a spell.*)

MRS CRUSOE
(*Hastily.*) Just a minute. Just a minute. I hope you know what you're
letting yourself in for?

DAVY
(*Pausing.*) Eh?

MRS CRUSOE
You wouldn't *believe* the trouble *I* had when *my* husband died. The *times*
I had to go into town. Twice to the *undertakers*, five to the *insurance*
office, three to the *probate* office, and dozens and dozens of *papers* to
sort out. By the time I'd finished, I was starting to wish he *hadn't* died.

DAVY
(*Annoyed.*) Aghhhh. (*Hurls his spell at them.*)

> (*Nothing happens. Everyone looks startled.* DAVY *tries
> again with the same result. He looks at his hands in
> amazement.*)

ROBINSON
(*Calmly.*) Something wrong?

DAVY
(*Shaken.*) Me magic powers have gone astray.

> (*Everyone brightens.*)

(*Snarls.*) But *don't* assume yer'll get away.
(*Draws his cutlass.*) With this, I'll chop yer in ter *pieces*
And *feed* 'em to the rats and meeces. (*Laughs harshly.*)

> (*All but* ROBINSON *fall back as he advances.*)

ROBINSON
(*Firmly.*) We'll see about *that*.

(*Snatches the Rod of Office from* Codine *and faces* Davy, *wielding it like a spear.*)

Davy
(*Amused.*) Yer thinks wi' *that*, yer'll win the fight?
Then come, young Crusoe . . . show yer might.

> (*He lunges at* Robinson, *who dodges the blow, and a fierce fight begins. The others cheer* Robinson *on. Suddenly,* Davy *howls, drop his cutlass and falls to his knees, C.F., clutching his arm.* Robinson *steps back, his spear aimed at* Davy's *chest. All cheer.* Disprin *hurries in up L. and runs to the* Queen's *side. They embrace.* Migranians *enter up L. and R., delightedly.*)

(*Moaning.*) I must be dreamin'. Them blows *hurt.*
He's cut me arm and ripped me shirt.
There's cuts an' scratches down me back,
An' bruises yellow, blue an' black.
Me muscles ache, as do me bones . . .
(*Wailing.*) But *nothing* can hurt Davy Jones. (*Sobs in misery.*)

Robinson
(*Pointedly reminding him.*) Except a *unicorn.*

Polly
(*Protesting.*) But there's no such thing, Robinson. He told us himself.

Robinson
True. But there is such a thing as a *sea* unicorn. I saw them *dozens* of times, when I was marooned on the *other* island. They're called *Narwals*, and look just like small whales, but have a single horn that grows through their upper lip. I realised *this* (*Shows the Rod of Office.*) was what Codine's Rod of Office was made from, only a minute ago, and thought it might just be the thing I needed to face up to *Mr Jones*, here.

> (*Enter* Fairy *down R. in her white light.*)

Fairy
And so it *was*. For Narwal horns are *from* King Neptune's unicorns . . .
And Davy's pow'rs, when *they* are near, just shrivel up and disappear.
So, Master Crusoe . . . take a bow. *You're* ruler of Migrania, now.

> (*Everyone reacts.*)

ROBINSON
(*Hastily.*) That's very *kind* of you, but the *last* thing I want is to rule *anywhere*. Queen Paracetamol would do a *far* better job. All *I* want, is to return home with Polly and the others, and get married.

SIR PERCY
(*Eagerly.*) And what about all this *treasure?* (*Indicates it.*)

FAIRY
It is, of course, King Neptune's claim.

(SIR PERCY *scowls.*)

Yet as this hero (*Indicates* ROBINSON.) . . . in *his* name . . .
Has fought and won. With due accord,
We offer him a small reward.
(*To* ROBINSON.) So as you soon intend to marry . . .
Take all the treasures you can carry.

(*All react with delight.*)

HALE
And what about him? (*Indicates* DAVY.)

HEARTY
Yes. You don't want *him* running round loose again.

BILLY
(*To audience.*) What shall we do with him, kids?

(*Audience suggestions as* DAVY *pleads for mercy.*)

ROBINSON
(*Stepping forward.*) Well they're all very good *suggestions*, but I think perhaps *King Neptune* should decide what to do with him.

FAIRY
Well spoken. And indeed he *will*. He'll cause old Davy tears to spill.
But now . . . by virtue of my power, to Hull you'll fly within the hour.
So choose your treasures, then away, to celebrate your Wedding Day.

(*All cheer. Music begins for . . .*)

MUSIC No. 18 (COMPANY)

(As they sing, Fairy *exits R., followed by a broken* Davy. *White and Green lights go out. At the end of the song, there is a rapid fade as the scene ends in celebration.)*

Scene Six: Back in Hull.

A lane scene. Can be as Act One, Scene Two, or a simple street scene. Full lighting. Enter Billy *L.*

Billy
Hiya, kids. (*Audience response.*) Ooooh, it's good to be home again. Only five *seconds*, and we were standing outside the front door with all the gold we could carry. A lot better than the *last* time I flew anywhere. What a *plane* that was. I won't say it was small . . . but we had to make a detour to spray a farmer's crops. And halfway across the Atlantic, the pilot came on the intercom and said they'd lost one of their *engines*. "But don't worry," he said. "We can still fly with three . . . but unfortunately we'll be an hour late." Ten minutes later, he was back again. "We've just lost another engine," he said. "But we can fly with two, only we're going to be *three* hours late." Half an hour later, we lost a *third* engine, "But it's no problem," he said. "We can fly with one, but we could be *six* hours late." Well . . . I was getting fed up with all this, so I complained to the air hostess. "If we lose *another* engine," I said, "We'll be stuck up here all night." Still . . . he was doing his best, I suppose, that pilot. When the other engine *did* go, he put on his parachute and went for help. Oh. but I must *tell* you . . . our Robinson's having a *marvellous* house built for us. It'll have all the latest gadgets in it . . . and every one of 'em *computerised*. (*Confidentially.*) I'm not keen on it, *myself*, though. I mean . . . how can you enjoy living in a house where even the light switch is brainier than you are? Here . . . and talking about houses . . . the minute we got home, old Sir Percy hired a Japanese cook and a German gardener. A week later, they got together and captured his house. (*He chortles.*) But we're all getting excited now. We're having the wedding in a few minutes, and me mum's doing all the arrangements. Ooooh, it isn't half going to be a *posh* do. No finger bowls on the tables for us. Me mum thinks they're dead common. So as soon as the meal's over, she's arranged for us all to go down to the Leisure Centre (*Or similar.*) to have a *shower*. The only trouble is . . . everybody in Hull's coming to the wedding . . . even Queen Paracetamol and the folks from Migrainia . . . so there's nobody left to sing in the choir. So I was *wondering* . . . (*Grins.*) I bet there's some *smashing* voices in here tonight. I know this lady in the front row (*Indicates vaguely.*) can sing, 'cos I've *heard* her. She's got a *huge* voice. In fact it's so big, the last time she sang at the Carol Concert, most of the audience had to leave to

make room for it. So how about it? Will *you* help us out for the wedding? (*Warning.*) You'll be here all night if you don't. We've still got *one* feller in the dressing room from *last* year's pantomime. (*Beaming.*) All right, then. I'll tell you what we'll do. I'm going to sing a little song, and after I've done it, I want to see if *you* can sing it any better. And if you *can* . . . *well* . . . you've got a place in the choir. So fellers . . . loosen your ties and undo your top buttons . . . and ladies . . . you can make your own arrangements.

MUSIC No. 19 (Billy)

> (*Community Song commences. If time permits, or if required,* Hale *and* Hearty *could assist with this. At the end of the song, he, or all, exit, and there is a rapid fade to end the scene.*)

Scene Seven: The Banqueting Hall of Crusoe Manor / Walkdown.

Full Set. A glittering hall inside Crusoe Manor. If possible, a small rostrum at the back with a short flight of steps leading down. Full lighting.

MUSIC No. 19 (Full Company)

> (*The walkdown commences as following, with everyone in eye-catching Finale costumes.*)

Chorus (*as* Citizens, Sailors *and* Migranians, *etc.*)
Dancers
Babes / Juniors
Codine *and* Disprin
Queen Paracetamol
Coral Fairy *and* Davy Jones
Sir Percy
Hale *and* Hearty
Billy
Mrs Crusoe
Robinson *and* Polly

> (*When the line up is complete, the music stops and the Final Couplets spoken.*)

Robinson
My new adventure's over, and my heart is filled with pride.

POLLY
Though troubles once beset us, I am now a blushing bride.

BILLY
So if you've had a giggle, and you'd ev'ry right to do so . . .

MRS CRUSOE
Tell all your friends to come along and see . . .

COMPANY
Robinson Crusoe.

> *(There is a reprise of the walk down song or another lively piece, then the FINAL CURTAIN FALLS.)*